A Note from the Autl

CW00665431

Welcome to the best-ever book of musical knowledge. It's particu....., ... practical exam syllabuses that require you to answer questions about the pieces you are playing, including Trinity College London's Musical Knowledge option (available as a supporting test at Grades 1 to 5) and the viva voce element of ABRSM diploma performance exams. It's also an essential musical knowledge resource for written exams up to GCSE and beyond!

This book assumes a basic knowledge of music notation. You will find information on:

★ Titles and their meanings

★ Terms and signs (including Italian, German and French terms)

★ More than 150 composers

★ Periods and styles of music

★ Keys and modulations

★ Form definitions

Every time you see this icon it means there are extra resources available on the website. Go to **www.blitzbooks.com** to download free worksheets, flashcards, manuscript and more! Obviously it's important to research your information from more than one source. On page 93 there is a list of excellent resources.

The most important thing about musical knowledge is that it should be just that - general music knowledge that you build up and use as part of your music education. Every time you learn something about a piece of music, you can usually apply that knowledge to another piece of music, which makes you a more informed musician.

Have fun with this book, and good luck with all your exams.

Samantha and Abe

Published by
Chester Music,
part of The Music Sales Group,
14-15 Berners Street,
London W1T 3LJ, UK.

Exclusive Distributors:
Music Sales Limited
Distribution Centre, Newmarket Road,
Bury St Edmunds, Suffolk IP33 3YB, UK.

Music Sales Pty Limited
4th floor, Lisgar House, 30-32 Carrington Street,
Sydney, NSW 2000, Australia.

Order No. CH85228
ISBN 978-1-78558-361-2

This pulp is from farmed sustainable forests
and was produced with special regard for the
environment. Throughout, the printing and binding
have been planned to ensure a sturdy, attractive
publication which should give years of enjoyment.
If your copy fails to meet our high standards,
please inform us and we will gladly replace it.

www.musicsales.com

Chester Music
part of The Music Sales Group
London / New York / Paris / Sydney / Copenhagen /
Berlin / Madrid / Hong Kong / Tokyo

Contents

$\longleftrightarrow$

CHAPTER 6: THE MAIN PERIODS IN MUSIC HISTORY

CHAPTER 7: KEYS AND MODES

CHAPTER 8: COMPOSERS

CHAPTER 9: PREPARATION FOR PRACTICAL EXAMS

CHAPTER 10: REFERENCES

Musical Knowledge in Practical Exams

WHAT YOU NEED TO KNOW

Many practical music exams consist of five main areas:

★ Technical work (scales, arpeggios, etc.)

★ Repertoire (your pieces)

★ Sight reading

★ Aural tests

★ **Musical knowledge**

The musical knowledge section is the bit where you get to show off everything you know about the pieces you're playing. The examiner asks all sorts of questions to check your understanding of the music. He/she will quiz you about some or all of the following:

★ Any of the terms and signs on the music

★ The key (including modulations), form and style of the piece

★ Information about the composer and other works written by that person

★ The period of music in which the piece was written

★ The meaning and/or significance of the title

Every syllabus and every grade is different. For early grades, like Initial or Grade 1, you may only be asked a few questions such as the key of the piece or the name of a note. In higher grades, you are expected to know much more. Knowing these things helps you to play the piece really well, because you have a deeper understanding.

Ask your teacher to check the syllabus for which things you need to know at your level. Don't forget: the higher the grade you're sitting, the more information you're expected to know. Refer to Chapters 9 and 10 for more exam hints and a list of suggested references.

Try not to leave your musical knowledge study to the last minute - it's too stressful! Use this book freely and frequently to build up your knowledge and to make sure it all stays in your head even after you finish playing your exam pieces.

How to Use This Book

'How to Blitz! Your Musical Knowledge' is a pretty general title! It's important for you to know exactly how this book will help you.

THIS BOOK CONTAINS INFORMATION ON:

★ Musical forms, titles and styles

★ Composers, foreign terms and general music terms

★ Exam time: how to prepare

The index at the back of this book is an extremely helpful tool. Look up anything you need to know. You can also go to **www.blitzbooks.com** for loads of extra information on a variety of musical knowledge topics.

THIS BOOK DOES NOT CONTAIN INFORMATION ON:

★ Pitch/note names

★ Metre/time signatures

★ General music notation (e.g. stems, rhythm grouping, etc.)

Your teacher will be able to explain everything you need to know about the actual notes on the page in your music. You can also go to **www.blitzbooks.com** for some great information sheets on note values and rhythms, as well as terms and signs for ABRSM Theory.

If you need information on things such as pitch names, time signatures or other aspects of music notation, you'll find almost everything you need to know in the 'How to Blitz!' series of theory books.

Musical Knowledge Questions

EARLY GRADES (Initial to approx. Grade 3)

The examiner may point to any aspect of the music and ask you a question about it. You must be able to:

- ★ explain the title
- ★ explain the key signature and time signature of the piece
- ★ name and explain all of the terms and signs on the page
- ★ describe the value of every note and rest

Below is a short piece of piano music followed by 10 questions relating to the 10 Roman numeral markings. This is a good example of the types of questions you may be asked in the early grades (answers page 92):

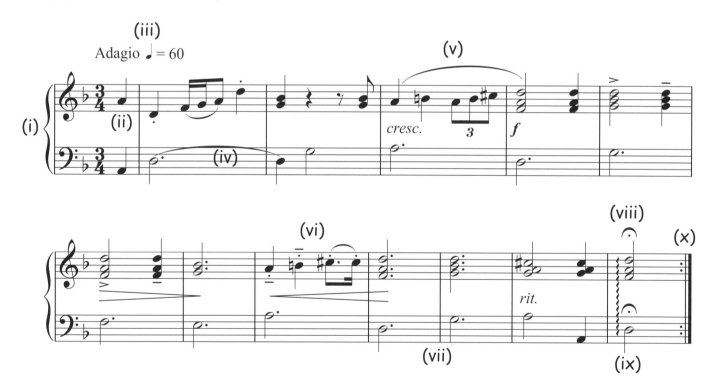

(i)   What is this curvy line at the beginning?

(ii)   Why is there only one beat in this bar?

(iii)   What does 'crotchet equals 60' refer to?

(iv)   What is this line connecting the two D notes?

(v)   What are these natural and sharp signs also known as?

(vi)   What are the dots, lines and slur on these notes showing?

(vii) What is this vertical line called?

(viii) What is this sign above this chord?

(ix) What is this squiggly line for?

(x) What are the dots at the end for?

Remember, you must know the meaning of EVERY term and sign on the page, even if you are not playing some of them as written, or playing from memory in the exam. Go through every tiny detail with your teacher as you learn the piece. (There are so many thousands of different signs in music that we could not possibly include them all here!)

If you have written the 'answers' on your music, make sure you rub them out before your exam!

INTERMEDIATE GRADES (approx. Grades 3-5)

For intermediate grades, you will need to:

★ know everything as you would for the early grades, including the meaning of the title, terms and signs, key signature and time signature

★ describe the form and the main modulations

★ comment on the style of the piece and the period in which it was written

Every syllabus and every grade is different. Make sure your teacher checks the syllabus to see the exact requirements for your exam.

HIGHER GRADES (approx. Grade 6 through to Diploma exams)

For higher grades, you are expected to be an expert on:

★ the piece itself: its form/structure, modulations, terms and signs

★ the composer: a little about his/her life story, other compositions, names of contemporaries

★ the period in which the piece was written, including other influences such as art, literature and painting.

For higher grades, this book will work for you as an initial reference, but you will need to do extended research on each of your composers and their pieces. Once again, make sure your teacher checks the syllabus to see the exact requirements for your exam.

How to Describe a Title

Every piece has a title, and usually the composer has specially selected that title to tell you something about the piece.

For your exam, you will be expected to know the meaning of the titles of all of your pieces. Some titles are purely descriptive, e.g. 'Walking Along'; other titles are named for their style or structure, e.g. 'Study' or 'Sonata'.

DESCRIPTIVE TITLES

Descriptive titles are those which describe an event, mood or emotion, rather than a type of musical structure.

For example, if your piece is called 'Sunny Day', you'll need to think about why the composer chose that name. Does the piece sound sunny? Does it make you feel the way you would on a sunny day?

If your piece is called 'Walking Along', it might get its title from an 'andante' tempo marking (meaning 'at an easy walking pace').

Here is a short list of pieces with descriptive titles, to give you an idea:

- The Vampire's Ball

- The Little White Donkey

- The Girl with the Flaxen Hair

- The Entertainer

- A Little Flower

- The Wild Horseman

- Mister Bumble

Descriptive titles can sometimes be tricky to explain, but as long as you give it a go and show that you've thought about the mood of the piece, you've done your job as a musician.

EXPLANATORY TITLES

Some titles refer to the form of the piece, e.g. 'Sonatina' (a small sonata), or the purpose of the piece, e.g. 'Study' (a piece written to improve technique). For these pieces, you need to understand the meaning of the title and how it relates specifically to that piece of music.

Here is a short list of some commonly found 'explanatory' titles, to give you an idea:

- Toccatina

- Sonatina

- Barcarolle

- Minuet

- Study

- Prelude

- Ecossaise

COMPOUND TITLES - A BIT OF BOTH

A 'compound' title is one that is both descriptive and explanatory.

Consider a piece called 'Homework Blues'. This sounds like a purely descriptive title, but the word 'blues' might indicate that the piece is based on a blues scale, or a 12-bar blues chord progression. You'll need to analyse your piece with your teacher to see whether the title takes its name from the 'blues' structure.

Now consider a piece called 'Nocturne', meaning 'night music'. This might appear to be purely descriptive as it does not really describe form or purpose. However, there were many 'Nocturnes' written in the 19th century and they all shared a reflective character and were usually free in form.

Definitions/explanations of some of these titles can be found in 'Common Musical Titles', beginning on the next page.

Common Musical Titles

One of the first questions an examiner may ask you is to describe the meaning of the title of your piece. We have made it easy for you by listing alphabetically all of the most commonly found musical titles. You can also refer to the index on page 94.

The first sentence or two of each definition is in **bold** type. This is the concise definition, which would be a suitable answer for the early grades. Most titles have more detail following the bold definition, which is excellent information to learn if you are doing a higher grade.

★　★　★

ALLEMANDE

Dance of German character and origin, most often in quadruple time.

'Allemande' is actually the French word for 'German'. The dance is stately and dignified in nature, and is usually in moderate tempo. It generally has continuous semiquaver movement, often with dotted quaver notes, and usually begins with an anacrusis. It is placed at the start of the Baroque Dance Suite or straight after the Prelude (see page 54).

AIR

Simple tune for voice or instrument.

ARABESQUE

Lyrical piece in which the main theme is presented in colourful and interesting ways.

An Arabesque is an ornate and decorative element in Arabian architecture. It is also a ballet position where the body is supported on one leg while the other leg is extended behind the body. Schumann was the first composer to use the term for a piece of music.

ARIA

Solo song within an opera or oratorio.

Aria in Italian means 'air' or 'song'. An Aria most often follows the recitative within an opera. The recitative carries the action of the story and is a speech-like song (see page 28), while the Aria, in contrast, has regular phrasing and melodic shape, expressing the character, feelings and reactions of the singer to the drama that may be unfolding.

ARIETTA

Short song or instrumental piece, simpler in character and structure than an Aria (see 'Aria' above).

ART SONG

Poem set to classical music, usually for trained voice and piano or orchestral accompaniment.

Art songs are vocal compositions with very refined artistic qualities in relation to the vocal line, text setting and sensitive accompaniment. They are composed with serious intent, in contrast to folk songs, for example. Such songs can be in any language, although English art songs, French 'Chansons', German 'Lieder', Spanish 'Canciones' and Italian 'Canzoni' are the most numerous (see also 'Lieder' page 21).

AUBADE

Song or instrumental composition referring to the early morning, rather than the evening.

Often an Aubade deals with the theme of lovers separating at dawn. An Aubade can also simply refer to a short instrumental piece.

BAGATELLE

Short composition, normally for the piano and usually in a light or whimsical style.

Bagatelle literally means a 'trifle'. Beethoven wrote 26 Bagatelles for piano, including the famous Für Elise.

BALLADE / BALLAD

Instrumental or vocal composition, popular in the 19th and 20th centuries. A Ballade usually tells a story.

A Ballade often has the character of an improvisation, and the style is usually dramatic. Chopin was one of the first masters to write Ballades for the piano. Brahms also wrote several Ballades.

BARCAROLLE

Boating song of the Venetian gondoliers, who were called the 'barcaruoli'. A Barcarolle is usually written in compound time.

A Barcarolle may also refer to any instrumental piece with the same gently undulating compound rhythm and lyrical beauty of the gondoliers' songs.

BAROQUE DANCE SUITE

Collection of dance music composed during the Baroque period (see page 54).

BERCEUSE

Cradle song or lullaby, or any instrumental piece with a very soothing atmosphere, normally in compound duple time.

Berceuse is French for 'lullaby', or cradle song. A Berceuse is usually in triple metre or compound metre. It is quite simple tonally, alternating between tonic and dominant harmonies. Frédéric Chopin's Op. 57 is a very famous Berceuse, written for solo piano.

BERGAMASCA / BERGAMASQUE

Italian peasant dance in quick 6/8 time.

The Bergamasca was named after an Italian city called Bergamo. It originally consisted of a specific harmonic progression over a ground bass (see page 49). A Bergamasca has the same lively energy as a Tarantella (see page 33). Some composers (like Debussy in his Suite Bergamasque) have used the term with very little reference to the original Bergamasca dance.

BOLERO

Latin music, generally in triple metre and with a slow or moderate tempo. It usually has a triplet on the second beat of each bar.

The Bolero originated in Spain in the late-18th century, and is a combination of two dances called the Contradanza and the Sevillana. Ravel's Boléro for orchestra (1928) made the dance especially popular.

BOOGIE / BOOGIE-WOOGIE

Lively style of blues piano in which the right hand plays over a continuous and repetitive left-hand pattern of driving quavers in the bass (often called an 'ostinato' bass).

'Boogie' was originally used to describe the faster, more energetic, percussive aspect of the blues style. Boogie follows exactly the same form and harmonic structure as the Blues (see page 41) but is faster and more joyful than Blues music. The characteristic use of straight quavers in the Boogie bass has given rise to the term 'eight to the bar'.

BOURRÉE

Lively dance of French or Spanish origin, usually in 2/4 or 4/4 time.

The Bourrée is much like the Gavotte, but starts on the 4th beat of the bar. It is one of the movements of the Baroque Dance Suite, often inserted between the Sarabande and the Gigue (see page 54). The Bourrée was also composed as an independent piece.

BURLESCA / BURLESQUE

Short piece with a lively, playful character.

BURLETTA / BURLA / BURLETTINA

Short comic Italian Opera; also a comic interlude within an opera.

Burletta in Italian means 'little joke'. The term was used in the 18th century to describe the comic interludes between the acts of a serious opera, while at times the term also applied to more extended works. In England, Burletta described works that parodied opera. Composers such as Max Reger and Béla Bartók have also used Burletta as a name for scherzo-like instrumental music.

CAKEWALK

Cakewalk music is usually in 2/4 time with syncopation and a heavy march rhythm.

The Cakewalk has its origins in dance music performed by African-Americans in the early 19th century. The dance developed from the 'Prize Walks' held in the days of slavery. The dancer with the most elaborate steps would win a cake (which is where the phrase 'taking the cake' comes from). The dance was performed in minstrel shows until the 1890s.

The music was adopted into the works of various composers, including John Philip Sousa and Claude Debussy. Debussy wrote 'Golliwog's Cakewalk' as the final movement of the Children's Corner suite.

> Remember, the first sentence or two of each definition, in bold, is the 'short' definition, suitable for early grades. The rest of the definition may be required in higher grades.

CANCIÓN

Canción in Spanish means 'song', and is characterised mainly by its melodic sweetness and expressiveness, usually in relation to the topic of love.

From the 14th to 16th centuries, the Canción was a very general term covering all the popular styles of vocal music in Spain that were not strictly religious.

CANON

Composition in which two or more identical parts begin at different times, like a round.

Each new voice enters at a specific point in the composition, and continues with the initial melody as the other voices enter, so that the voices continually overlap each other. If the imitation is exact in every detail, then the Canon is called 'strict'. If any changes appear in the imitation, then it is a 'free Canon'.

CANTATA

Extended choral work, usually of a religious nature, and set for solo voice or voices and chorus, often with an orchestral accompaniment.

The term Cantata comes from the Italian verb 'cantare' meaning 'to sing'. In the 17th century, Cantatas were set to both religious and secular texts and became quite complex and elaborate compositions. Bach wrote approximately 300 Cantatas, which he scored for soloists, chorus and orchestra.

CANZONA / CANZONE / CANZON

Vocal or instrumental piece based on a vocal form.

Canzona comes from 'chanson', the French word for 'song', and it describes several types of music composition. In the 16th century it was often used to describe a polyphonic French song or a polyphonic vocal arrangement set to a poem. By the 17th century, a Canzona was a solo song with keyboard accompaniment, or simply an instrumental piece or movement in the style of a song.

CAPRICCIO

Like a short Caprice (see above), and generally suggests a lively piece of music with unexpected effects.

The Capriccio originated as a popular dance in the late-16th and 17th centuries in the style of a free-form Fugue (see Fugue, page 56). Composers like Janáček and Stravinsky wrote Capriccios for piano and orchestra. Capriccios have also been written solely for the orchestra, as in Tchaikovsky's Capriccio Italien.

CAPRICE

A short, fast instrumental piece, with playful effects.

The most famous Caprices are the 24 that Paganini wrote for violin. He created whimsical effects and surprises with regard to melody, rhythm, modulation and form.

CAVATINA

Lyrical instrumental piece; also an operatic solo aria.

When Cavatina refers to an operatic aria, it normally describes an aria that has only one section without any repetitions, rather than the traditional three sections. Cavatina can also describe a simple melodious air. Beethoven's String Quartet in B♭ Op. 130 has a Cavatina movement.

CHACONNE

Old and gentle dance of Spanish origin, usually in triple time.

The Chaconne is similar to the Passacaglia (see page 26). Both are generally in triple time and consist of a melody or a set of variations above a Ground Bass (where a theme in the bass is repeated throughout the piece - see page 49). The Chaconne is one of the less standard movements of the Baroque Dance Suite (see page 54). A famous Chaconne appears in Bach's 2nd Partita for solo violin.

CHORALE

Hymn tune of the Lutheran or German Protestant Church, and usually sung in unison.

Martin Luther compiled a great many melodies and texts that could be sung with ease by the congregation. These melodies were the basis for organ compositions and church cantatas during the 17th and 18th centuries. Bach composed about 30 Chorales and re-harmonised about 400 existing Chorale melodies, arranging them in four parts for singing by trained choirs.

CHORALE PRELUDE

Elaborate organ composition based on a hymn tune and probably one of the most important types of organ composition of the Baroque period.

The Chorale Prelude originated in 17th-century Germany as an organ introduction to a hymn to be sung in the Lutheran Church. Chorale Preludes were often in variation form and always in contrapuntal style. Bach wrote 143 Chorale Preludes in four-part harmony.

CODA

The closing section of a piece or movement.

Coda means 'tail' in Italian. It is often used to reinforce the sense of the tonic key towards the end of a piece. The Coda may use ideas that have been introduced earlier in the piece, or may contain brand new thematic material – such as the rather exciting Codas in many of Beethoven's symphonies.

CODETTA

Literally 'short Coda'; concludes the middle section of a piece.

In a Fugue, the Codetta is a brief episodic passage between two Subject entries during the Exposition (see Fugue, page 56).

CONCERTO

Extended work in three or four movements in which a solo instrument features against an orchestra.

See also page 37.

CONGA

Latin-American line dance featuring three steps and a kick on the fourth beat of the bar.

CONSOLATION

Six pieces for solo pianoforte by Liszt, composed in 1850.

The pieces are said to have been inspired by a set of poems by the French poet Charles Augustin Sainte-Beuve. Consolation No.3 in D♭ major is possibly the most well known of Liszt's Consolations.

Remember, the first sentence or two of each definition, in bold, is the 'short' definition, suitable for early grades. The rest of the definition may be required in higher grades.

COURANTE / CORRENTE

Fast dance of French origin in triple time.

Courante literally means 'running'. This is reflected in the lively rhythm and character of the piece, which consists of mainly quaver or semiquaver movement. There are two types of Courante. The French form often mixes simple triple with compound duple rhythms –

the last bar of each section being in 6/4. The Italian form, called 'Corrente', is a little faster than the French Courante, and generally consists of a fluid, running upper line and supporting bass line. Both the French and Italian forms are regular dances found in a Baroque Dance Suite (see page 54), and both start with a short anacrusis.

DA CAPO ARIA

Aria in three-part (Ternary) form, in which the third part is a repetition of the first.

The Da Capo Aria was very popular in the Baroque period. It was sung by a soloist and accompanied by a small orchestra.

DIVERTIMENTO

Popular form in the 18th century that was identical to the Classical Serenade - a suite of several movements played by a chamber group or small orchestra.

Divertmento means 'amusement' or 'entertainment' in Italian. The Divertimento was lighter in style than the Baroque Dance Suite. It was often intended for outdoor performance and aimed at being purely recreational and entertaining. The movements in a Divertimento may include minuets, marches and movements in Sonata form. Mozart and Haydn wrote many Divertimentos.

ECOSSAISE

Lively dance of Scottish origin in 2/4 time.

Ecossaise means 'Scottish dance' in French. It was introduced to France at the end of the 18th century. The Ecossaise is normally in 2/4 time and rather quick in tempo. Beethoven, Chopin and Schubert all wrote Ecossaises for the piano.

ELEGY / ÉLÉGIE

Song of lament for the dead, or one that suggests a melancholy event.

ENTR'ACTE

Music played between acts of a play or an opera.

Probably the best-known Entr'actes are Schubert's Entr'actes for Rosamunde.

ETUDE / STUDY

Etude is French for 'study'. This is music which has been written with the intent of improving the performer's technical ability.

Usually an Etude will focus on just one or two specific technical challenges, such as octave work or fast-running passages. Composers such as Chopin, Liszt and Debussy wrote Etudes that were musical masterpieces as well as technical training pieces.

FANDANGO

Lively Spanish dance in simple triple or compound duple time.

Despite the fast tempo of the Fandango, it is marked by sudden stops during which the dancing couples remain motionless, and at times sing. The Fandango is generally accompanied by guitar and castanets.

FANFARE

Short piece of music often composed for brass instruments, usually played at the start of a very formal ceremony.

FANTASIE / FANTASIA

Fantasie in Italian means 'whim' or 'fancy'. Most Fantasies have unexpected changes of mood and style throughout the piece, to give the impression that the performer is improvising.

Many Fantasies were fugal in nature with alternating sections of rapid passagework. Composers of Fantasies were more concerned with freedom of expression than rules regarding structure and form. In the 19th century, Schumann, Chopin and others used the term 'Fantasy' to refer to short mood pieces composed without the constraints of Sonata form.

FOLK SONG

Song with no known composer and which is often passed down through the generations without being written down.

Folk songs became an important part of the national culture in the 19th century, when many composers such as Grieg, Dvořák, Bartók and Tchaikovsky used them as the basis for many of their compositions.

FORLANA

Lively northern Italian dance in 6/4 or 6/8 with repeated motifs.

The Forlana flourished in the early 18th century as a French court dance, after which it gained popularity in Venice with gondoliers and 'street people'. Stylised Forlanas include those in Bach's Suite No.1 for orchestra and Ravel's Le Tombeau de Couperin.

FRENCH OVERTURE

An early form of orchestral operatic overture, popular in the 17th and 18th centuries.

It opened with a slow movement, which ended in a quick fugal section. This was followed by a short dance movement – often a Minuet.

FUGHETTA

Short Fugue, or piece of music in the style of a Fugue (see Fugue below).

FUGUE

Composition for several voices or parts (generally three or four). Most popular in the Baroque period, and mainly written for keyboard instruments at that time. A Fugue is built on a very formal structure, using much imitation between the parts or voices.

Fugue in Latin means 'flying after'. It is the effect of the various voices following each other, or 'flying' after each other - that gives the piece its distinctive title. The theme, or 'Subject' of the Fugue is introduced at the beginning of the piece in one part only, and the other voices enter successively in imitation of each other within a very formal structure. (See page 56 for more information on Fugue terms.)

GALLIARD

Lively dance in triple time, dating back to the 15th century.

The Galliard was often paired with the slower Pavane (see page 27) to provide contrast. The Galliard dance was quite athletic, characterised by vigorous leaps, jumps and hops.

GALOP

Quick German dance in 2/4 time.

The Galop was popular as a ballroom round dance throughout Europe in the 19th century. It involves a little hop or a change of step at the end of each phrase.

GAVOTTE

A rhythmic and sprightly French dance in 2/2 or 4/4 time.

The Gavotte generally features a half-bar anacrusis and is a regular component of the Baroque Dance Suite (see page 54). The Gavotte is usually taken at a moderate to fast tempo.

GIGUE / JIG

A dance in compound time, often contrapuntal in style and nearly always used as the final dance of the Baroque Dance Suite (see page 54).

Associated with Scotland and Ireland, the English 'Jig' comes from the French 'Gigue', which means small fiddle or 'giga'. The Gigue is fast and energetic, usually has a short anacrusis and is in compound triple metre; however, it is occasionally found in 3/8, or even 4/4 where it has a dotted-note rhythm.

GREGORIAN CHANT

This was the official music of the Roman Catholic Church for over a thousand years, and was synonymous with Plainsong (see page 27). See also Pre-Baroque music, page 69.

HABAÑERA

A slow dance in 2/4 time, originating in Havana, Cuba.

One of the most famous Habañeras is found in Bizet's opera Carmen.

HUMORESQUE / HUMORESKE

Short, lively, whimsical piece.

This title was often used by Dvořák and Schumann to describe their pieces.

HYMN

Religious song in praise of God, often set to a poem.

Hymns are strongly associated with the Christian church, especially where hymnal melodies are a regular part of the church service.

IMPROMPTU

Music of the Romantic era which gives the feeling of spontaneity or improvisation.

Impromptu in French means 'improvised' or 'on the spur of the moment'. In the 19th century, Impromptus often had a song-like quality, featuring a lyrical melodic line. Schubert wrote eight famous Impromptus.

Remember, the first sentence or two of each definition, in bold, is the 'short' definition, suitable for early grades. The rest of the definition may be required in higher grades.

INTERMEZZO

A short and light musical piece, originally performed between acts of a drama or opera.

The title 'Intermezzo' is interchangeable with Interlude or Entr'acte. By the early 18th century, intermezzos began to be performed as independent pieces, although the term still applies to instrumental interludes between acts of a play or opera for example. The most famous piano Intermezzos are by Brahms and Schumann.

INVENTION

Name given by Johann Sebastian Bach to 15 short compositions where a specific theme or motif is shared between two or three voices and is imitated and developed in various ways.

Bach's 15 two-part Inventions are probably best-known, but he also composed 15 three-part Inventions which he called 'Sinfonias' (these are quite different to the 'Sinfonias' found in the Baroque Dance Suite). 'Invention' suggests a composition that came about not merely through inspiration, but through being carefully crafted piece by piece, like a real construction or invention.

ITALIAN OVERTURE

Type of overture which gained popularity during the 17th and 18th centuries.

The Italian Overture was characterised by a three-movement structure (quick/slow/quick), and was the predecessor of the Classical symphony.

LIEDER

Plural of 'Lied', which is German for 'song'. In Lieder the words and accompanying music are of equal importance.

During the Romantic period, Lieder took their lyrics from the outstanding poets of the period, like Goethe and Hesse. The accompaniment demanded as much refined artistic interpretation as the melody, both reflecting very carefully the meaning of the underlying poetry. The most prolific composer of Lieder was Franz Schubert, who wrote over 600 songs.

LOURE

Old dance in 6/4 time, generally slow and strongly accented.

The Loure was one of the movements of a Baroque Dance Suite (see page 54).

LULLABY

A soothing song, usually sung to children before they go to sleep.

Lullabies written by established classical composers are often given the name Berceuse (see page 12). One of the most famous lullabies of all is Brahms' Wiegenlied.

MADRIGAL

Vocal composition for several voices, generally unaccompanied.

First sung in Italy during the 14th century, Madrigals experienced a peak of popularity in the 16th century, at which time they were mostly written in five parts and in a highly imitative, polyphonic style. They are usually set to pastoral, satirical or amorous texts.

MALAGUEÑA

Spanish dance originating in Malaga, a coastal town in southern Spain.

The melody of a Malagueña is always very rich and usually has a guitar accompaniment with a typically Spanish feel. The Malagueña, as a piano solo, tries to recreate the sense of both singer and guitar accompanist. The music is closely related to the Fandango – a type of dance that became very popular in Spain during the 18th century (see page 18).

MAMBO

Latin-American-style dance using rhythms derived from African folk music.

The Mambo also features elements from European music such as the Spanish 'contradanza'.

MARCH

Composition in 4/4 or 2/4 time, designed for rhythmic accompaniment to marching.

A March can also be a stylised performance piece rather than a real marching piece. March tempo is usually 112–120 beats per minute. The form of a March is generally in three sections, the second normally being a little more lyrical, with the third being a repeat of the first section. Slower March tempos are normally more suggestive of bereavement and funeral processions, e.g. Chopin's famous Funeral March.

MASS

Formal religious ceremony that commemorates the Last Supper by consecrating bread and wine.

The Mass has provided a rich setting for much music composition over the centuries. The five passages that are frequently set for choirs are: 1. Kyrie (Lord Have Mercy);

2. Gloria in Excelsis Deo (Glory be to God on High); 3. Credo (I Believe); 4. Sanctus (Holy, Holy); 5. Agnus Dei (O Lamb of God).

Bach's Mass in B minor and Beethoven's Mass in D are examples of how composers have utilized the Mass to create musical masterpieces.

MAZURKA

Traditional Polish dance in triple time.

Mazurkas normally have two or four sections, each of eight bars. The phrases often have a slight accentuation on the second or third beat of each bar, and there is much use of dotted notes. Chopin wrote over 60 Mazurkas for the piano and was the first composer to introduce this form as a serious part of the performance repertoire.

MÉLODIE

French song in which the words and accompanying music are of equal importance. It is the French equivalent of the German 'Lied' (see page 21).

MINUET / MENUET / MINUETTO / MENUETTO

A stately French dance in 3/4 time.

Dating back to the 17th century, the Minuet is usually in moderate tempo and in triple time, and begins on the first beat of the bar (although towards the 18th century an anacrusis became more fashionable). The Minuet was almost always included as one of the main dance movements in the Baroque Dance Suite, placed between the Sarabande and Gigue (see page 54). It was an extremely popular dance in the court of King Louis XIV of France. The Minuet dance consisted of small dainty steps ('menu' means 'small' in French). By the late-18th century, composers such as Mozart and Haydn started including the Minuet in many of their sonatas and symphonies, and soon added a middle section called the Trio, which was followed by a repeat of the initial Minuet.

MINUET AND TRIO

Common third movement of a Sonata, Symphony or Concerto.

In the Classical period, the Minuet and Trio became a popular form for the third movement in larger works such as symphonies and sonatas. The Minuet was followed by a Trio, which was then followed by a repeat of the initial Minuet (see also Minuet above, Minuet and Trio Form on page 37 and Trio, page 34). The Trio was so called because composers would often write them in three-part harmony, or they reduced the number of performers to three (usually two oboes and a bassoon). The name Trio remained, even when all traces of this orchestration had vanished. The Trio usually provides some form of contrast to the Minuet by means of different key and orchestration.

MOTET

Vocal composition generally set to sacred texts.

Motets were very popular from the 13th century onwards. During the Baroque period, Motets were imitative in style and were generally set for unaccompanied voices (solo, choir or both) singing sacred Latin texts. Palestrina wrote about 180 Motets.

MUSETTE

Type of rustic dance with a repetitive drone bass suggesting the bagpipes.

A Musette was also a type of French bagpipe popular in court circles during the 17th and 18th centuries.

NOCTURNE

Tranquil, quiet piece. Nocturne means relating to the night.

A Nocturne is a piece, usually composed for piano, which evokes the special atmosphere of dusk or nightfall, with its gentle tranquility and also with its more restless and troubled moments. It generally has a song-like melody over an arpeggiated accompaniment. The Irish composer John Field was the first to popularise the term, and he is often regarded as the father of the Romantic nocturne. The most famous exponent of the form was Frédéric Chopin, who wrote 19 Nocturnes. Debussy wrote three orchestral pieces called Nocturnes.

NOVELETTE

Composition for piano which suggests a story. In old Italian, 'novella' means 'piece of news' or 'tale'.

Novelettes are generally quite free in form and thematic material. Schumann, Poulenc and Heller all wrote Novelettes.

OPERA

Dramatic work in which the greater part of the text is sung. An opera includes all aspects of performance: scenery, costumes and dramatic action.

An Opera requires the singers to be in full costume. There are sets and orchestral accompaniment and much importance is placed on the quality of the acting, not just the singing.

> Remember, the first sentence or two of each definition, in bold, is the 'short' definition, suitable for early grades. The rest of the definition may be required in higher grades.

OPERETTA

'Little' opera, with a light atmosphere.

An Operetta has more dialogue and makes more of the comic aspects than an Opera. It may include popular songs and dances, added to the production to boost audience appeal. This less serious version of Opera developed during the 19th century, a good example being the Operettas of Gilbert and Sullivan.

ORATORIO

Extended work for soloists, chorus, and orchestra on a dramatised Biblical text.

In contrast to opera, Oratorio is normally presented without scenery or costumes. In the late-16th century, St Philip Neri established the performance of sacred plays with music which took place in the oratory (small chapel) of the Vallicella Church, in Rome.

OVERTURE

An orchestral introduction to an opera, play or oratorio.

Gluck was the first composer to create a thematic link between the overture and the work that followed it. Beethoven did much to make the form popular.

PART SONG

Vocal composition, often unaccompanied, with the melody in the highest part, and accompanying harmonies in the other voices.

Part Songs were very popular in the 19th century, with beautiful and enduring songs composed by Weber, Schubert, Mendelssohn, Schumann, Gounod, Brahms, Liszt and many others.

PARTITA

In the 17th century, the term 'Partita' referred to a variation, but by the 18th

century, it was used to describe a Baroque Dance Suite (see page 54).

The main difference between a typical Baroque Dance Suite and a Partita is that the latter has a much larger proportion of non-standard movements, or 'Galanterien', than the Suite. Some Partitas do not even have the four main dances of the standard Baroque Dance Suite. Bach wrote six keyboard Partitas (often called German Suites) and three for solo violin. His keyboard Partitas are considered more weighty and heavy than his French and English keyboard suites. The following dances appear in at least one or more of Bach's six keyboard Partitas: Prelude, Praeambulum, Ouverture, Fantasia, Sinfonia, Toccata, Allemande, Courante/Corrente, Aria, Sarabande, Gavotta, Minuet, Rondeau, Capriccio, Burlesca, Passepied, Gigue.

PASSACAGLIA

Old, slow dance of Spanish origin.

The Passacaglia is extremely similar to the Chaconne (see page 15). Both are generally in triple time and consist of a melody or a set of variations above a Ground Bass (where a theme in the bass is repeated throughout the piece). The term Passacaglia probably derives from the Spanish pasacalle, which means 'street song'. The Passacaglia is one of the less standard movements of the Baroque Dance Suite (see page 54).

PASSEPIED

Lively old French dance in either 6/8 or 3/8 time, resembling a quick minuet.

Passepied in French means 'pass-foot', referring to one of the steps in the dance. It is one of the less standard movements of the Baroque Dance Suite (see page 54).

PASSION

Very similar to an Oratorio but dealing specifically with the Passion of Christ according to the Gospels (see Oratorio page 25).

The 'Passion' of Christ refers to the events and suffering – physical, spiritual, and mental – of Jesus in the hours prior to and including his trial and execution by crucifixion. Passions are normally performed during Holy Week, the week before Easter.

PASTORALE / PASTORAL

Instrumental or vocal composition suggesting a tranquil country scene, generally in compound time.

Beethoven wrote two famous pieces that both evoke a pastoral atmosphere: the Pastoral Sonata (Op. 28 in D major) and Pastoral Symphony (Op. 68 in F major).

PAVANE / PAVAN / PAVANA

Tender, dignified dance in duple time, usually in three sections.

The Pavane was originally an Italian dance that later became popular in Spain.

PLAINSONG

This was the official music of the Roman Catholic Church for over a thousand years.

From 590-604 AD, Pope Gregory the First reorganised the set prayers of the Catholic Church, as well as the huge body of Plainsong (also called Gregorian Chant - see page 20) that had been evolving over many centuries. It was based on the Church Modes (see Modes page 82) and was sung in Latin, in unison and without accompaniment. Plainsong had no time signatures or bar lines and moved mainly by step with very few leaps.

POLKA

Bohemian dance in moderately quick 2/4 time.

The Polka's popularity spread throughout Europe during the early 19th century.

POLONAISE

National Polish dance in triple time, believed to have originated in the 16th century.

The Polonaise is somewhat slower than the Waltz, and usually consists of two or three sections. The Polonaise was one of the non-standard movements of the Baroque Dance Suite (see page 54), featuring syncopation and phrases often ending on the third beat of the bar. Handel, Mozart, Beethoven, Weber and Schubert all wrote Polonaises. Chopin transformed the Polonaise to become a dramatic showpiece. His 10 Polonaises for the piano are technically very demanding.

PRAEAMBULUM

Introductory movement in a Baroque Dance Suite, similar to a Prelude.

Bach's keyboard Partita No. 5 in G major opens with a Praeambulum.

PRELUDE

The Baroque Prelude preceded or introduced a larger work, establishing the mood and key of the work that followed. In the 19th century a Prelude was an independent piece.

Preludes were often used as first movements of Baroque Dance Suites (see page 54), or as orchestral introductions to operas, or they were followed by Fugues (see Fugue page 19 and page 56, and Well-Tempered Clavier page 35). Bach also wrote some independent preludes.

Towards the 19th century the title Prelude was used by composers such as Chopin, Rachmaninoff and Debussy for self-contained, independent compositions. They were short pieces which often 'painted a picture' or described a fleeting or specific emotion.

QUADRILLE

Type of French square dance normally with five sections.

The Quadrille was popular in the early 19th century and was later introduced into Britain. The five sections were usually set in 6/8 and 2/4 time alternately. The music was adapted from popular tunes, operatic arias, and even sacred works. It was danced by two or four couples.

RECITATIVE

Style of singing in opera which lies somewhere between speech and song.

Recitative makes use of the natural rhythms of speech. It is used in opera and oratorio, and its function is to carry the action of the story forward. There are two main types of Recitative: secco and stromento (or 'accompagnato'). The first type, secco (meaning 'dry' in Italian), has very little accompaniment – only occasional arpeggiated chords, generally played by harpsichord. Stromento has a fuller orchestral accompaniment with instrumental passages often inserted between the vocal phrases.

REQUIEM

Musical setting of the Mass for the dead, originally sung in the Roman Catholic Church.

The title 'Requiem' (Latin for 'rest') comes from the opening words of the text in the Requiem mass: 'Requiem aeternam dona eis, Domine'. There have been many beautiful settings of the Requiem Mass by composers such as Mozart, Berlioz, Verdi and others.

REVERIE

Instrumental composition suggestive of a dreamy or musing state.

RHAPSODY

Piece featuring a strong heroic or epic nature.

Rhapsodies are often charged with a robust energy and exhibit sharply contrasting moods. Popular national or folk melodies may be woven into the composition. The title first became popular in the 19th century when Liszt wrote his Hungarian Rhapsodies. There are many orchestral Rhapsodies, while Brahms used the term for solo pianoforte compositions and for his Alto Rhapsody for male chorus and orchestra.

RICERCARE

Elaborate contrapuntal composition often in 4/2 time, in fugal or canonic style.

The Ricercare was popular from the 16th to the 18th century. In Bach's Musical Offering the Ricercare takes the form of a Fugue in six parts (see Fugue page 56, and Canon page 14).

RIGAUDON / RIGADOON

Very old and sprightly French dance in duple or quadruple time.

The Rigaudon originated in Provence. By the late-17th century, it started appearing in the Baroque Dance Suite (see page 54) and in French Operas. It is similar to a Bourrée, but the Rigaudon is rhythmically simpler. It is thought that the name of the dance comes from a Marseille dance master, Rigaud, who introduced the dance to Parisian society in 1630.

Remember, the first sentence or two of each definition, in bold, is the 'short' definition, suitable for early grades. The rest of the definition may be required in higher grades.

ROMANZA / ROMANCE / ROMANZE

General name given to a lyrical, tender or romantic song, or an instrumental piece in the style of a romantic song.

RONDEAU

French instrumental piece in which the verse and refrain are repeated according to a very strict pattern.

The Rondeau dates back to the Renaissance period and is distinct from the 18th-century Rondo, although the use of recurring thematic material is an important part of both. It is one of the less-standard movements of the Baroque Dance Suite (see page 54). Bach included a Rondeau in his Partita No. 2 for keyboard.

RONDO

Instrumental form that originates from the old 'round dance', and has the main theme recurring several times throughout the piece.

Rondos usually have a fast and vivacious character. Usually in Rondo form (see page 38), the main theme alternates with one or more contrasting themes and recurs in the same key at least three times.

ROUND

Canon in which each part returns to the start again and again after reaching the end of the melody (see page 14).

A round may also be called an 'infinite canon'. Three Blind Mice is an excellent example.

RUMBA / RHUMBA

Fast Latin-American dance, normally in 8/8 (3+3+2).

SAMBA

Relaxed and flowing Latin-American dance in 2/4 time with syncopated patterns.

The Samba is a combination of the African Mesemba dance and Brazilian Maxixe. The term applies to a variety of things: a large Samba percussion group, a Samba jam session, and also to an intensely polyrhythmic style of drumming. Jobim's famous One Note Samba is a perfect example of this gentle style.

SARABANDE

Slow and stately dance of Spanish origin in triple time.

The Sarabande is normally in 3/2 or 3/4 time and starts without an anacrusis. It often has a long note or emphasis on the second beat of the bar. It has a homophonic texture (i.e. based on chords) and features many ornaments. The Sarabande usually appears as the third dance in a Baroque Dance Suite (see page 54).

SCHERZINO / SCHERZETTO

Short Scherzo (see below).

SCHERZO

Literally meaning 'joke' in Italian, a Scherzo is a light-hearted, playful type of piece.

It was originally a term used for both vocal and instrumental compositions before 1750, after which it was used to name the third movement of a sonata or symphony – often taking the place of the Minuet. Like the Minuet it is in triple time, but much faster and more whimsical and playful. Haydn was the first composer to start tampering with the Minuet, giving it a much more carefree feel. Beethoven took this to far greater lengths, transforming the sober Minuet into a Scherzo with an exuberant and playful character. The Scherzo was almost always combined with a Trio, in much the same way as the original Minuet had been. Beethoven included the Scherzo & Trio as a regular movement in extended works such as sonatas and symphonies.

SERENADE

Evening music; in the vocal tradition, a love song sometimes sung beneath a lady's window, with guitar or mandolin accompaniment.

In 18th-century instrumental music, the term Serenade was used much like the Divertimento, to describe a suite of several movements played by a chamber orchestra. The Serenade was lighter in style than the Baroque Dance Suite.

SERENATA

Dramatic cantata of the 18th century.

A Serenata is like a short opera, and deals with secular rather than religious themes. The term also can mean a Serenade (see above).

SICILIANO

Slow dance, often in a minor key and written in compound time, either 6/8 or 12/8.

The Siciliano is of Sicilian origin and often evokes a pastoral atmosphere. It is one of the less standard movements of the Baroque Dance Suite (see page 54). The Siciliano is also a slow vocal aria in the style of a Sicilian folk song.

SINFONIA

Literally means 'symphony'. Bach used the term for his three-part Inventions (see page 21).

In the 17th and 18th centuries, a Sinfonia was an orchestral piece which served as an introduction to an opera, suite or cantata.

SONATA (Baroque)

Solo instrumental piece in several movements, often with 'basso continuo' accompaniment.

See also Sonata da Camera and Sonata da Chiesa on page 38.

SONATA (Classical)

Solo instrumental piece in 3-4 movements where the first movement is in Sonata form.

The word Sonata comes from the Italian verb 'sonare', meaning 'to sound'. The first movement is almost always in Sonata form (see page 55). The exact structure of Sonata form (also called 'first movement form'), was firmly established in the Classical period by composers such as Haydn and Mozart, and the form continued to be used by most composers throughout the Classical and Romantic periods. Large orchestral works like symphonies and concertos generally follow the same form as the Sonata.

SONATINA

Short Sonata, slightly less structured and technically easier than the Sonata.

The great masters composed Sonatinas as preparatory pieces for their own students to help them understand the demands of the more complex and sophisticated Sonatas. As a result, most Sonatinas lack passages and ornaments that are technically demanding, and they may at times have as few as two movements. However, some Sonatinas composed in the 20th century (e.g. by Ravel, Milhaud and Sculthorpe) are in fact quite difficult to play.

Remember, the first sentence or two of each definition, in bold, is the 'short' definition, suitable for early grades. The rest of the definition may be required in higher grades.

SONG WITHOUT WORDS / LIEDER OHNE WORTE

Term introduced by Mendelssohn for a short pianoforte solo that has the character of a song with accompaniment.

Mendelssohn wrote 48 Songs without Words.

SPIRITUAL

Religious song of the African-American people.

The melody of a Spiritual is generally simple in style and often has syncopated rhythms. Standard themes are of death, resurrection, release from suffering and the final homecoming to the promised land. Spirituals became very popular in the 1870s. Swing Low, Sweet Chariot and Deep River are two well-known examples.

STUDY / ETUDE

A piece of music written to improve technique.

Usually a Study will focus on just one or two specific technical challenges, such as octave work or fast-running passages. See also Etude, page 17.

SUITE

A composition made up of a group of dance movements or short pieces. See also Baroque Dance Suite, page 54.

SYMPHONY

Large-scale orchestral composition, in three or four movements, generally following the same form as a Sonata (see page 55).

It was during the Classical period especially that the modern symphony crystallised. Joseph Haydn is considered to be the 'father of the modern symphony', sculpting it into its standard form of four movements.

TAMBOURIN

Lively music in duple time, in imitation of a tambourin drum.

Tambourin refers to an old type of French drum. It was also a popular dance during the 18th century. Many examples of the Tambourin exist in the music of Jean-Philippe Rameau, usually scored with a piccolo solo.

TANGO

Moderately slow dance in 2/4 or 4/4 time, usually involving dotted rhythms.

The Tango is originally from Argentina and became popular throughout Europe and the United States in the early 1900s. It usually employs dotted rhythms like the Habañera (see page 20) and is characterised by gentle syncopation.

TARANTELLA

Fast Neapolitan dance with a strong rhythmic drive, usually in 3/8 or 6/8 time.

It is said that the venomous bite of the tarantula spider in Taranto (from where the dance originates) causes the victim to dance frenetically, which ironically is also the cure for the venomous bite. Chopin, Rossini, Liszt and Mendelssohn all wrote Tarantellas.

THEME AND VARIATIONS / AIR AND VARIATIONS

Form in which a theme is stated and then reintroduced several times with variations.

The changes or variations may take place in the melody, rhythm, tonality, texture, tempo, harmony, or combinations of all these. At first, this form was used within a larger piece, e.g. one movement of a Sonata or Symphony, but it subsequently became a popular form in its own right.

TOCCATA

Virtuosic keyboard piece intended to demonstrate the performer's dexterity and ability to manage a variety of 'touches' on the keyboard.

Toccata in Italian means 'touched'. The organ composers of the early 17th century developed the form, and Bach made it famous through his harpsichord and organ Toccatas, especially the Toccata and Fugue in D minor for organ.

TOCCATINA

Short, less technically demanding Toccata (see above).

TOMBEAU

Title used by French composers in the 17th century for a lament or memorial on the death of a notable person.

Tombeau in French means 'tomb' or 'tombstone'. In Ravel's Le Tombeau de Couperin, the composer dedicates the six movements to the memory of six of his friends who died fighting in World War I.

TRIO

Middle section of the 'Minuet and Trio' movement (see Minuet and Trio Form page 37 and Scherzo page 30).

The Trio usually provides some form of contrast to the Minuet or surrounding movements by means of a change of key and different orchestration. The Trio was so called because it was originally written for a group of three performers. The most common combinations are the string trio (violin, viola, cello) and the piano trio (piano, violin, cello).

VOCALISE

Vocal composition without words, which is sung on one or more vowel sounds.

Vocalise often refers to vocal exercises, but it can also apply to concert works or even to sections of a larger composition. Rachmaninoff's Vocalise Op. 34 No. 14, is a well-known example of Vocalise.

WALTZ

Dance in 3/4 time, most popular in Vienna during the 19th century.

The Waltz probably originated from the Ländler, a German folk dance. Waltzes range from being serious and reflective (such as those by Brahms and Chopin), to those that are light and entertaining (such as the Viennese Waltzes of Johann Strauss).

WELL-TEMPERED CLAVIER

The Well-Tempered Clavier (The 48) is a set of 48 Preludes and Fugues by J.S. Bach.
Bach composed 'The 48' for any keyboard instrument of the time ('Clavier' means keyboard). It is called 'Well-Tempered' because it demonstrated the use of a new tuning system that was suitable for all 24 keys.

Up until Bach's time, the tuning system in use was the 'mean-tone' system. This problematic system of tuning was based on an acoustic perfect 5th (i.e. the 5th that is produced naturally as a harmonic when the main note has been played). The acoustic perfect 5th was a slightly smaller interval than the perfect 5th we hear on pianos today. The 5th on keyboards of that time sounded fine in one key, but not in another key, and enharmonic notes did not always share the same pitch, i.e. F♯ did not sound the same as G♭.

In practice, this meant that keyboards had to be retuned every time there was a piece in a different key. This was very inconvenient, as sometimes it would be necessary in the middle of a concert!

Bach was one of many composers who strove to devise a new way of tuning keyboards that would solve this problem. Tuning systems developed from the 'mean-tone' system to 'well-tempered' and finally to 'equal temperament', which was used to tune all keyboards from the mid-19th century.

With equal temperament, the octave is divided into 12 equal semitones. These intervals are not acoustically perfect but are close enough that the ear cannot really notice the difference.

In 1722, Bach decided he would demonstrate to the musical world the advantages of a 'well-tempered' keyboard (which was slightly less exact than equal temperament) by composing a Prelude and Fugue in each of the 12 major and minor keys. Bach's demonstration proved to be a great success and, in 1744, he composed another 24 Preludes and Fugues. The whole collection is often referred to as 'Bach's 48'.

(See also; Prelude, page 27 and Fugue, page 56.)

ZORTZICO

Folk dance from the Basque region of Spain, usually in 5/4 time, with dotted notes on beats 2 and 4.

Common Musical Forms

⟷

With the exception of Rounded Binary form (listed under Binary) and Compound Ternary form (listed under Ternary), these forms are listed alphabetically, and once again the first sentence or two is in bold to give you a brief summary of the definition. Remember to refer to the index on page 94 if you can't find what you're looking for in this chapter.

★ ★ ★

BAR FORM

Often used to describe the AA-B structure.

The form originated from an old German style of vocal composition called the Minnelied. Here, the opening phrase or 'Stollen' is repeated (A-A) and then followed by a contrasting one (B), the 'Abgesang' (aftersong).

BINARY FORM: A-B or AA-BB or A-BB

Music divided into two parts (often called Two-Part Form).

The first section generally ends in the dominant key (or the relative major if the piece is in a minor key). The second section starts in the new key and generally does not contrast greatly with the first section (unlike Ternary form). Section B always ends in the tonic and does not have to be the same length as the first part.

When the two sections are repeated one or more times (AB - AB - AB), this is just called Double Binary or Extended Binary. If the form is AA-B, then this is called Bar form (see above).

ROUNDED BINARY FORM: A-BA or AA-BA

Music essentially in two parts with a brief and modified return of the A section.

This looks and sounds very much like Ternary form but there are some important differences. In Rounded Binary form, the first A section finishes in a related key or on chord V of the tonic key, i.e. with an imperfect cadence, while in Ternary form the first A section finishes with a perfect cadence in the tonic key. The B section in Rounded Binary form may share some features with the A section, while in Ternary form, the B section contrasts sharply with the A section. In Rounded Binary, the A section is usually abbreviated when it is restated after the B section.

CONCERTINO

Short and light concerto (see below) for solo instrument and orchestra.

A good example of a concertino is Weber's Clarinet Concertino, Op. 26.

CONCERTO

Extended work in three or four movements in which a solo instrument features against an orchestra.

Concerto comes from the Latin 'Concertare', meaning to compete or discuss – referring to the dialogue between soloist and orchestra. Concertos have also been written for more than just one instrument to feature against the orchestra. The form of the Concerto is much the same as the Sonata (see page 55), and its form and style were established primarily by Mozart. The Concerto not only presents an unfolding drama between soloist and orchestra, but it also showcases the individuality and importance of the solo instrument and exploits the virtuosity of the performing artist.

CONCERTO GROSSO

A Baroque orchestral work in three movements with sections for a group of two or three solo instruments ('concertino') in dialogue with the full orchestra ('ripieno' or 'tutti').

The two instrumental groups alternate with each other in a lively and colourful dialogue. Concerto Grosso was the most important form of Baroque orchestral music, good examples being Bach's Brandenburg Concertos Nos. 2, 4 and 5.

MINUET AND TRIO FORM

Movement in Compound Ternary form consisting of the Minuet and Trio.

In the Classical period, the Minuet and Trio became a popular form for the third movement in larger works such as symphonies, concertos and sonatas. The Minuet was followed by a Trio, which was then followed by a repeat of the original Minuet.

The Trio was so called because some composers wrote it in three-part harmony, or reduced the number of performers to three. The name Trio remained, even after all traces of orchestration had vanished. The Trio usually provided some form of contrast to the Minuet by means of a change of key and different orchestration.

Because each part of the Minuet-Trio-Minuet is in Binary form, the name for the overall form of the movement is more correctly called Compound Ternary form rather than just Ternary form.

RONDO FORM: A-B-A-C-A

Usually in five sections, the main theme (A) sounding at least three times and separated by two contrasting sections (B and C).

Rondos usually have a fast and vivacious character. In Rondo form a main theme alternates with one or more contrasting themes and recurs in the same key at least three times. A very famous example of Rondo form is Beethoven's Für Elise. For a piece to be in Rondo form the two contrasting sections must be different from each other. If both contrasting sections are the same, the form is A B A B A - which is Extended Ternary form.

MODIFIED STROPHIC FORM

Modified Strophic form relates to art song and Lieder. It has a similar musical setting for most stanzas, and usually features one or more contrasting sections.

This form is suitable for poems with a consistent theme throughout but which may have one or two stanzas with a change in mood. Schubert's Der Lindenbaum is a good example.

RITORNELLO FORM: Tutti-Solo-Tutti-Solo-Tutti-Solo etc.

An early type of Rondo form, where the main theme returns in different keys.

The whole orchestra ('tutti') opens with the main theme (the 'ritornello' or refrain) which is repeated between solo passages, each time in a different key. This form was quite popular with Bach and Handel, and evolved into Rondo form by the Classical period.

SONATA FORM

See page 55.

SONATA DA CAMERA

Secular (non-religious) chamber Sonata, popular in the Baroque period.

The Sonata da Camera had several dance-like movements for two or three string players and keyboard accompaniment. Corelli did much to promote the Sonata da Camera.

SONATA DA CHIESA

Church Sonata, popular in the Baroque period.

The Sonata da Chiesa had four movements (slow-fast-slow-fast) and was set for two or three string players with an organ accompaniment. It was intended as a performance piece during church services.

SONATA-RONDO FORM: A-B-A-C-A-B + CODA

Sonata-Rondo form (or Rondo-Sonata form) is the result of two different forms or structures combining, i.e Sonata form (see page 55) and Rondo form (see page 38).

In Sonata-Rondo form, the main theme appears at the start of the Exposition, then again at the start of what might loosely be called the Development, and once more at the start of the Recapitulation. This means that the main Theme returns at least three times, which is a fundamental requirement of Rondo form. In Sonata-Rondo form, the crucial difference is that the Second Subject group appears in the dominant key first, and then finally reappears at the end in the tonic key, just as the Second Subject would do in Sonata form.

Composers have certainly modified the form in subtle ways, but the crucial thing to remember is that the main Theme is woven into the overall structure so that it appears at least three times.

For a more detailed explanation and diagram go to **www.blitzbooks.com**

32-BAR SONG FORM: AA-B-A

Commonly used for popular song-writing. There are four eight-bar sections making an AA-B-A pattern (this is essentially Ternary form - see next page).

The A sections end with a perfect cadence in the tonic key. The B section is also called the Bridge, and often modulates to different keys. It ends on chord V of the tonic key, which prepares for the return of the A section.

Two-part Song form consists of an opening melody followed by a second, contrasting melody. This is the same as Binary form.

SONG CYCLE

Group of poems by one poet, set to music by one composer, and referring to a particular theme.

The Song Cycle gained great appeal during the 19th century. The songs within the cycle all have a central idea or mood and usually a sequence of songs that tell a story. Both Schubert and Schumann wrote some very beautiful Song Cycles, e.g. Winterreise by Schubert.

Remember, the first sentence or two of each definition, in bold, is the 'short' definition, suitable for early grades. The rest of the definition may be required in higher grades.

STROPHIC FORM

Strophic form relates to Art Song and Lieder. It has the same theme and accompaniment repeated for each verse, with only very minor changes.

The Strophic song is suited to poems that have the same mood or atmosphere throughout.

TERNARY FORM: A-B-A

Music in three sections in which both A sections conclude with V-I in tonic key.

In Ternary form, the first section should be complete in itself, ending with a perfect cadence in the tonic key. The middle section (often called an Episode) provides sharp contrast with the outer sections in terms of key and/or melodic material. The last section (i.e. the repeat of A) ends with a perfect cadence in the tonic key. The instruction 'da capo al fine' at the end of a B section will always transform a piece from Binary to Ternary form, and here the A sections are identical. When the return of A is varied, the form is often outlined as A-B-A1.

A-B-A-B-A is called Extended Ternary form. If the form is A-B-C without a return to A, this is called Three-Part form rather than Ternary form.

COMPOUND TERNARY FORM: A-B-A

Music in three sections in which each part has its own form.

This occurs when each of the three sections of Ternary form have their own independent form – either Binary or Ternary. A good example is the Minuet-Trio-Minuet, where each of the three sections is in Binary form.

THEME AND VARIATIONS / AIR AND VARIATIONS

Form in which a theme is stated and then reintroduced several times with variations.

The changes or variations may take place in the melody, rhythm, tonality, texture, tempo, harmony, or combinations of all these. At first, this form was used within a larger piece, e.g. one movement of a Sonata or Symphony, but it subsequently became a popular form in its own right.

THROUGH-COMPOSED / DURCHKOMPONIERT

Relating to Art Song and Lieder, a form in which the musical setting changes for each verse according to the mood of the poem.

The continual changes in a Through-Composed song tend to give the work a very dynamic and dramatic quality. Schubert's The Erl-King is a good example of this type of composition.

Definitions of Styles

There are many different ways to describe style in music - it all depends on how much detail you want to go into. The following definitions are quite concise and would be suitable answers at most exam levels. Go to the index on page 94 if you are not sure whether the term you are looking for falls into this section.

For high-level practical exams, you should research the styles in which you are playing and be able to describe each in great detail, with examples of other pieces composed in that style. Go to **www.blitzbooks.com** for extended definitions of many of these styles.

★   ★   ★

A CAPPELLA

Literally 'in the style of the church'; music written for one or more vocalists performing without instrumental accompaniment of any kind.

ATONAL

Music that is written and performed without regard to any specific key, often with deliberate dissonances, sometimes with an aim to shock the audience.

BAROQUE

Music composed during or in the style of the Baroque period. See page 70 for a full description.

BLUES / 12-BAR BLUES

Blues is a unique style of vocal or instrumental music. It is usually played at a moderately slow tempo to portray the 'blue' (sad) mood of the songs. Blues music follows a specific chord progression which is often called 12-Bar Blues form. The 12 bars are divided into a pattern of tonic, subdominant and dominant harmonies, over which the soloist improvises a melody using notes from the Blues scale.

The 12-Bar Blues chord progression consists of 12 bars in three phrases:

I – I – I – I

IV – IV – I – I

V – IV – I – I

The minor Blues scale beginning on C is as follows: C - E flat - F - F sharp - G - B flat - C.

BOOGIE / BOOGIE-WOOGIE

Percussive, rhythmic and lively style of blues piano in which the right hand plays over a continuous and repetitive pattern of driving quavers in the bass (often called an 'ostinato' bass).

'Boogie', was originally used to describe the faster, more energetic, percussive aspect of the blues style. Boogie follows exactly the same form and harmonic structure as the Blues (see Blues, above) but is faster and more joyful than Blues music. The characteristic use of straight quavers in the Boogie bass has given rise to the term 'eight to the bar'.

BOSSA NOVA

Bossa Nova in Portuguese means 'new beat'. It is a slower form of the Samba, with cool jazz elements, and with the melody shifted to lead guitar (see Samba page 30).

Bossa Nova became popular in the United States and Europe in the 1960s. The music is generally set in minor modes, conveying a mood of longing and melancholy. One of the best examples of the Bossa Nova style is Antônio Carlos Jobim's The Girl from Ipanema.

CLASSICAL

Music composed during or in the style of the Classical period. See page 72 for a full description.

EXPRESSIONISM

A violent and often atonal style of music used as a means of evoking heightened emotions and states of mind.

FUGATO

This describes a section of music treated in fugal style, even though the piece as a whole is not actually a Fugue (see Fugue page 19 and page 56).

IMPRESSIONIST

Music composed during or in the style of the Impressionist period. See page 76 for a full description.

INDETERMINATE / INDETERMINACY

Also known as 'Chance Composition' or 'Chance Music'. The composer distances themself from actually choosing the notes and uses dice or other such means to create the music randomly.

JAZZ

Modern style characterised by improvisation, syncopation, and chords with added 7ths, 9ths, 11ths, etc.

Jazz has its roots in early 19th century America, in the blues music and work songs of the cotton plantations. It developed through the 1900s and now encompasses many different styles such as blues, bebop, swing, Dixieland, soul, cool, funk and fusion. Throughout the modern era the word 'jazz' has come to mean music that is separate from traditional classical music but distinct from pop and rock.

LATIN-AMERICAN

Music that originates from Latin-American countries such as Brazil, Cuba and Argentina. Some Latin-American music, like Bossa Nova, is strongly influenced by American Jazz.

Latin-American music has complex and syncopated rhythmic qualities and features percussion instruments such as bongos, maracas, guiros, cabazas and claves. Some Latin-American music is defined by particular dance styles, e.g. Tango, Mambo and Samba (see Chapter 2).

MINIMALIST

Also known as 'minimalism', this refers to compositions based on extremely short musical ideas or motifs, which are developed throughout the composition by minimal changes e.g. very small adjustments over a long period of time. Minimalist compositions are typically very long and often test an audience's concentration.

MODAL

Based on one of the seven church modes (see page 82).

MODERN / 20TH CENTURY

A general term referring to music composed after about 1900. See page 78 for a full description.

NATIONALISM

Late Romantic/early modern style, in which strong ties to their country inspired composers to write music based on folk tunes and anthems, particularly in Hungary and Germany.

NEO (e.g. Neo-Classical, Neo-Romantic)

Music written some time after the period but having stylistic characteristics of that period.

POP

Pop music encompasses a wide range of stylistic features. 'Pop' literally comes from 'popular' and describes music that is immensely popular for a limited period of time, and which appeals to youth culture in particular. Pop music may represent the sentiments and feelings of a particular period; as the era passes into history, so does the music. Some pop songs and pop performers have had enduring popularity, appealing to several generations, such as the music of the Beatles and ABBA.

RAGTIME

Syncopated piano music generally in duple or quadruple time, popular in America from the 1890s to the 1930s.

The term Ragtime suggests that the timing or meter has been 'ragged' and torn apart by the heavy emphasis on syncopation. While the 'oom-pah' bass is very rhythmic and predictable, the syncopated melody line continually displaces strong accents and long notes to the weaker beats.

A typical Rag has four sections, each one being 16 bars in length. Scott Joplin was the most famous Ragtime composer.

RENAISSANCE

Music composed during the period before the Baroque era. See page 69 for a full description.

ROCK AND ROLL

Style of popular music that developed in the early 1950s as a result of the fusion of black rhythm and blues music with white country and western music.

Rock music generally has a strong beat and a prominent vocal melody line. It is accompanied primarily by drums and guitar (bass, rhythm and lead), and depends heavily on the guitar sound for its character. The chord progressions usually centre around chords I, IV and V. Bill Haley & His Comets' recording, Rock Around the Clock in 1955 was one of the first big Rock and Roll hits.

ROCK BALLAD / POP BALLAD

Like the classical ballad, a Rock or Pop Ballad is based on telling a story. While the classical ballad suggests a story through music, the Rock ballad actually tells one, with words. It can be dramatic, even funny, but most Rock Ballads are slow and romantic. Two well-known examples are Jimmy Webb's MacArthur Park and Don McLean's American Pie.

ROCOCO STYLE / STYLE GALANTE

A light, ornate and elaborate style that developed in France in the first part of the 18th century and influenced many areas of artistic expression.

Rococo contrasts with the preceding heavier, grandiose Baroque style. In music, this new Rococo style was called Style Galante. (See also Early Classical, page 72)

ROMANTIC

Music composed during or in the style of the Romantic period. See page 74 for a full description.

SERIALISM / 12-TONE MUSIC

A composition based on a set sequence of the 12 notes in an octave, each used once only. This sequence is known as the 'tone row'.

 For more detailed information about many of these styles, visit **www.blitzbooks.com**

General Terms

←——————————————————————→

The following alphabetical list of definitions covers general music terminology. We've tried to cover the most common music definitions but it would be impossible to include absolutely everything! If you can't find what you're looking for here, it may be listed under **Common Musical Titles** beginning on page 10, or **Common Musical Forms** beginning on page 36. Plus you can always check in the index on page 94 for instant directions!

Definitions of rudimentary things such as sharp/flat/natural signs, repeat signs, pause, accents, etc. are not included in this book. These are fully explained in How to Blitz! ABRSM Theory Grades 1-3. You can also go to **www.blitzbooks.com** to download a great list of terms and signs.

Remember to go through your pieces with your teacher to make sure you understand all the terms and signs on the page. For a comprehensive list of Italian, French and German terms, see Chapter 5 beginning on page 59.

★ ★ ★

Acciaccatura

Commonly found ornament also known as a 'crushed' note; grace note with no rhythmic value of its own, played at the same time as or just before the main note.

Accidental

Sharp, flat or natural sign appearing during the piece rather than in the key signature (also applies to double sharps and double flats).

Ad libitum (ad lib.)

Latin term meaning 'at pleasure', 'quite freely'.

Alberti Bass

Type of bass line made up of a triad broken into a 'bottom-top-middle-top' pattern, e.g. 𝄢♩♩♩♩ . It is so called because the Italian composer Domenico Alberti used it so often in his harpsichord sonatas.

Alla Breve

Two minims per bar, often called cut common time; usually suggests a faster tempo than 4/4.

Anacrusis

Incomplete bar containing one or more unaccented beats before the first bar line.

Appoggiatura

Grace note played on the beat with the main note sounding after. It often takes half or two-thirds of the rhythmic value of the main note.

Basso Continuo

An accompaniment created from a bass line and numbers indicating chord positions, known as a 'figured bass'. Prominent in the Baroque period.

Brace

Curved line used to group the two staves for keyboard playing. →

Bracket

Used to group multiple staves into a single system, for ensemble score-writing.

BWV

Abbreviation of 'Bach Werke-Verzeichnis'; the catalogue system used to index J.S. Bach's works.

Cadence

Sequence of chords (usually just two) that ends a phrase, either in the middle or the end of a composition, providing harmonic 'punctuation' to the piece.

Cadenza

Originally an improvised cadence by a soloist, it later became a written passage to display the virtuoso skills of the performer. It usually occurs towards the end of a movement in a concerto.

Canon

Like a round; composition in which two or more identical parts begin at different times.

Chalumeau Register

The lowest octave on the clarinet, beginning on bottom E. It has a full and reedy tone.

Chamber Music

Instrumental music for a small group of instrumentalists, originally intended for a more intimate performance in a room rather than a church or theatre. In Chamber Music each part is played by only one instrumentalist. The string quartet, for example, is considered to be typical Chamber Music and consists of two violins, viola and cello, with all parts being given equal importance.

Chorus

Has three meanings: 1. Group of singers; 2. The singers in an opera who do not have a solo part; 3. The important and repeated sections of a popular song (see also Refrain, page 51).

Chromatic

Has two meanings: 1. Scale progressing in semitones only, including all twelve notes of an octave; 2. Phrase in which there are two or more notes with the same letter name.

Coda

The closing section of a piece or movement.

Codetta

Small coda which concludes a section of a piece.

Contrapuntal

Involving counterpoint; polyphonic.

Counterpoint

Two or more melodic lines played at the same time, each with equal importance, often involving imitation.

D or DV

Abbreviation of 'Deutsch Verzeichnis', the catalogue system used to index Schubert's pieces.

Development

Middle section of an extended movement such as in a Sonata, in which the musical themes and melodies are developed. (See also Sonata, page 55).

Diatonic

Has three meanings: 1. Based on a major or minor scale; 2. Interval coming from such a scale; 3. Phrase in which all notes have a different letter name.

Dominant

Fifth note/degree of the scale; key based on fifth degree of the scale.

Double Stopping

Bowing two strings at once (relating to stringed instruments).

Duet

Composition for two performers, each having equal importance.

Dynamics

Words or signs that indicate the levels of volume in a composition, e.g. 'p' or 'ff'.

Enharmonic

Two notes that have the same sound but a different name, e.g. C sharp and D flat.

Equal Temperament

Tuning system developed in the late Baroque period in which the octave is divided into 12 equal semitones. (See Well-Tempered Clavier, page 35.)

Exposition

The opening section of an extended movement, such as in a Sonata. Sometimes referred to as the 'enunciation'. (See Sonata, page 55, and Fugue, page 56.)

Figured Bass

Numbers/figures under a bass line indicating the harmony and inversions of the chords.

Fundamental

The first note in the harmonic series, from which overtones can be achieved.

Glissando

Sliding between two notes any distance apart. Sometimes referred to as 'portamento' in relation to singing.

Ground Bass / Basso Ostinato

Short motif in the bass that is constantly repeated throughout a composition with varying treatment of the harmony and melodic line.

Harmonic

Note from the harmonic series achieved by overblowing (wind instruments) or touching the string lightly at a certain point, allowing the string to vibrate at a higher frequency.

Hob.

Abbreviation of 'Hoboken', the catalogue system used to index Joseph Haydn's works. Anthony van Hoboken was the Dutch musicologist who catalogued all of Haydn's works in 1957.

Homophonic

From the Greek, meaning 'sounding alike'; a style emphasising a single harmonised melody line, often termed as the opposite to polyphonic.

HWV

Abbreviation of 'Händel-Werke-Verzeichnis', the catalogue system used to index G.F. Handel's works.

K or KV

Abbreviation of 'Köchel Verzeichnis', the catalogue system used to index Mozart's pieces. Ludwig von Köchel gave each of Mozart's pieces a Köchel number in 1862.

Key Signature

The flats and sharps at the beginning of each staff indicating the key of the music.

Leitmotif

German term meaning a recurring motif given to a particular idea or main character of an opera. Developed mainly by Wagner.

Libretto

The text of a vocal work, particularly opera.

M.M.

'Maelzel's Metronome' (the metronome was invented by Johann Maelzel in 1815). 'M.M. ♩ = 60' would mean the metronome should be set to beat out 60 crotchet beats per minute. A common interpretation of the meaning of M.M. is 'metronome marking'.

Mode

Usually refers to the 'Church Modes' used in the Middle Ages (see page 82).

Modulation

Change of key (see page 80).

Motif

Melodic figure developed throughout a composition.

Moto Perpetuo

Meaning 'perpetual motion'; term used for a very fast instrumental piece that continues in short note values throughout. Latin term 'perpetuum mobile' also used.

Opus (Op.)

Latin term meaning a work or collection of works. Used by composers to chronologically catalogue their works. If the opus consists of more than one piece, there is a numeric extension, e.g. 'Op. 25, No. 3'. 'Opus posthumous' (Op. posth.) indicates the work was published after the composer's death.

Ornament
Sign indicating the embellishment of a note, for example a turn, trill, upper mordent or lower mordent.

Ostinato
A repeated phrase, often forming the bass line of a composition. Ostinato in Italian means 'stubborn', pointing to the insistence of the continually repeating musical figure. When the repeated figure is in the bass, it is called a Basso Ostinato or Ground Bass.

Pedal Point
A repeated or sustained note, often the tonic or dominant, usually occurring over several bars and often in the bass (see also Fugue, page 56). The term dates back to the time when the main keyboard instrument was the pipe organ, which had a separate pedal keyboard for the organist's feet.

Pentatonic Scale
Five-note scale often used by jazz musicians and in folk music. The major pentatonic scale is made up of scale degrees 1, 2, 3, 5 and 6 of the major scale. The minor pentatonic scale is made up of scale degrees 1, 3, 4, 5 and 7 of the natural minor scale.

Period
Section of music consisting of two phrases, often four or eight bars long each. The first phrase usually ends with an imperfect cadence, while the second ends with a perfect cadence.

Polyphonic
Literally 'many sounds'; also known as Contrapuntal, a style combining two or more independent parts.

Polytonality
Two or more key signatures functioning at the same time.

Recapitulation
Concluding section of an extended movement such as in a Sonata or Fugue in which themes are revisited. (See Sonata, page 55 and Fugue, page 56.)

Refrain
A repeating phrase at the end of each verse in a song, sometimes referred to as the chorus.

Relative Major/Minor

Key with the same key signature but opposite tonality (see also Key Relationships, page 80).

Round

Like a canon; composition in which two or more identical parts begin at different times.

Sequence

The immediate repetition of a musical passage at a higher or lower pitch from the original. There are two main types of sequences: real and tonal. In a real sequence, the repeated section is an exact transposition of the original, including the harmonic structure. If the sequence has been altered, it is called a tonal sequence.

Subdominant

Fourth note/degree of the scale; key based on fourth degree of the scale.

Subject

Main theme or motif in an extended work such as a Sonata or Fugue (see Sonata, page 55 and Fugue, page 56).

Syncopation

The stressing of beats or pulses that are normally weak, often producing a jazz-like effect.

Tacet

Latin term meaning 'silent', often used when orchestral instruments have long periods of not playing.

Theme

Main musical idea, often developed with variations.

Tierce de Picardie/Picardy 3rd

Term applied to a major 3rd used at the final cadence point of a piece (or section of a piece) which is otherwise in a minor key. The sudden change in tonality can have a brightening effect on the music. The origin of the term 'Picardy' is unknown.

Tonality

Usually referred to as the major or minor quality of a composition or scale.

Tonic

First note/degree of the scale; key based on first degree of the scale.

Tremolo

Quick repetition of the same note (string playing) or the rapid alternation between two notes.

Trill

Rapid alternation between two adjacent notes.

Tutti

Passage for the entire ensemble or orchestra without a soloist.

Variations

Small movements following and developing a theme.

Vibrato

Vibrating on the note using breath (voice, woodwind, brass) or hand movements (strings) to create a strongly reverberating note.

Whole-tone scale

Six-note scale consisting entirely of tones (whole-tone steps).

WoO

Abbreviation of 'Werke ohne Opuszahl', which is German for 'work without opus number'. A catalogue term applied to the 205 works of Beethoven that lack opus numbers. Many of these compositions were published during Beethoven's lifetime, but he did not feel they were worthy of an opus number.

The Baroque Dance Suite

The simple definition of a Suite is that it is a collection of dance music composed during the Baroque period.

Each dance within a Suite is in the same key set for that Suite, and each is in Binary form with both parts repeated. Every dance has its own distinct characteristics; you can find descriptions of each dance (listed alphabetically) in Chapter 2, beginning on page 10.

Most suites include four core dances originating from various parts of Europe:

★ Allemande (from Germany)

★ Courante / Corrente (from either France or Italy)

★ Sarabande (from Spain)

★ Gigue (from England, Ireland or Scotland)

Other dances were often added to the four core dances and these were usually inserted between the Sarabande and the Gigue. These extras were referred to as the 'Galanterien' and included dances such as:

★ Minuet (included so often it was sometimes considered to be a core dance)

★ Prelude

★ Gavotte

★ Loure

★ Air

★ Bourrée

Once again, each of these dances is described in Chapter 2.

Bach, Purcell and Handel were probably the most prolific composers of the Dance Suite. Bach wrote (for keyboard) six French Suites, six English Suites, and six German Suites called 'Partitas' (see page 25). The French Suites are characteristically very graceful and light in style. The 'English' Suites were so called because the original manuscript describes the work as 'Fait Pour les Anglais' - 'Made for the English'. Bach's keyboard Partitas are considered more weighty and heavy than his French and English keyboard Suites.

The Classical Sonata

A Classical Sonata is a solo instrumental piece in three or four movements where the first movement in particular follows a very strict form or structure known as Sonata form.

If you are playing a Sonata in your exam, you will need to understand the structure of Sonata form. Even if the particular movement you are playing is not in Sonata form, you should still understand where the term comes from (see page 31).

A movement composed in Sonata form follows a strict formula. It has three main sections: Exposition, Development and Recapitulation, and it may or may not feature a Coda. Your teacher will help you find how the following description relates to the Sonata you are playing.

Exposition

In the Exposition, there are usually two main themes, the 'First Subject' and a contrasting 'Second Subject'. These two subjects are often connected by a passage called a 'bridge', 'link' or 'transition'.

The First Subject is always stated in the **tonic** key. The Second Subject is always in a related key, usually the **dominant**. If the Sonata is in a minor key, the Second Subject is usually in the relative major key. The Exposition ends in the key of the Second Subject.

Development

The Development section is where new themes may be presented, or fragments of the previous Subjects are developed in various ways and usually through a number of different keys (usually related keys such as the relative minor or the subdominant - see Key Relationships, page 80). The Development often has a contrasting mood.

Recapitulation

The concluding section, the Recapitulation, is generally a repeat of the Exposition, but here the 1st and 2nd Subjects are both in the tonic key.

SONATA FORM AT A GLANCE

Exposition (A): First Subject **tonic** key ⟶ Second Subject **dominant** key

Development (B): Subject material developed in different keys

Recapitulation (A): First and Second Subject in **tonic** key

---

The Fugue

←——————————→

A Fugue is a composition for several voices or parts (generally three or four). Fugue is Latin for 'flying after', referring to the effect of the various voices following each other or 'flying after' each other. It was most popular in the Baroque period and followed a very formal structure using much imitation between the parts or voices.

You will need to be familiar with all of the terms listed here if you are playing a Baroque Fugue in your exam. Your teacher will help you find examples of each term in your piece. Following this list of fugal terms is a detailed description of the three sections in a Fugue. (See also Fugue, page 19, Well-Tempered Clavier, page 35 and Prelude, page 27.)

Subject

A melody that comprises the primary melodic/rhythmic material of the Fugue. It generally consists of two halves: the 'head', which often has adventurous intervals or rhythms, and the 'tail' which is more step-wise and steady in rhythm.

Answer

An imitation of the Subject that immediately follows the initial statement of the Subject. The Answer is always in a different voice and is usually a 5th higher or a 4th lower.

A fugue with an Answer that is an exact transposition of the Subject (a 'Real Answer') is called a **Real Fugue**. A fugue with an Answer that has some intervals adjusted (a 'Tonal Answer') is called a **Tonal Fugue**.

Countersubject

A melody that appears in counterpoint to the Subject. It first appears as a continuation of the Subject in the same part (while the Answer has already started). The Countersubject then reappears as an accompaniment of the principal theme - whether Subject or Answer - until the Exposition is complete.

Augmentation

The lengthening of the original time values of the Subject, often found towards the end of the Fugue, adding dignity and impressiveness to the theme.

Diminution

The shrinking of the original time values of the Subject, often creating a sense of tension, urgency and forward motion.

Coda

The concluding section of a Fugue. The Coda generally consists of imitative work based on the Subject material. It often features Stretto (see below), it may visit the Subject one last time (usually in the bass voice) and it often employs a Pedal Point (see below).

Codetta

A brief passage between two Subject entries during the Exposition. The Codetta often helps bring back the tonality to the tonic key, especially if the Answer has just been stated in the dominant. Not all Fugues have Codettas.

Inversion

Melodic inversion occurs when the Subject material is rewritten 'upside down', like a mirror image: ascending intervals become descending, 3rds become 6ths, and so on.

Counter-Exposition

A second exposition following the initial exposition, in which the voices enter in a different order. When all the parts are employed, the Counter-Exposition is said to be 'complete'. If one or more parts is absent, it is 'incomplete'.

Episode

A small section or phrase introducing new material, or using fragments of the Subject material. Episodes almost always appear in the Modulatory section.

Mutation

This may also be called 'change of mode'. It involves a re-statement of the Subject or Answer in the opposite tonality (e.g. major to minor) of its original statement.

Pedal Point

The repetition of a bass note or notes, usually the tonic or dominant, over several bars, irrespective of the harmonies in the treble clef above.

Sequence

Repetition of a motive or melodic fragment at another pitch level, usually up or down a step. Each repetition is called a 'leg'.

Stretto

The overlapping of thematic material. This occurs when the second part enters before the first part has completed its statement of the subject. This creates a build-up of tension and forward motion.

Invertible Counterpoint

A way of writing two voices so that they can swap positions with each other on the stave – the higher voice can become the lower voice and vice versa, without breaking the strict 18th-century conventions of contrapuntal writing.

THE STRUCTURE OF THE FUGUE

The Exposition, or Enunciation

The Exposition features the orderly sequential entry of the main theme, known as the 'Subject', in each and every voice. The Subject is usually unaccompanied the first time it is introduced. It is then repeated in a different voice, starting a fifth higher or fourth lower, and this is called the Answer. If the Answer has been modified in any way (for example, an interval might change from a 4th in the Subject to a 5th in the Answer), then the Fugue is said to be a 'Tonal Fugue'. If the Answer is a direct transposition of the Subject, then it is called a 'Real Fugue'.

The Answer is always heard with an accompanying melody played by another voice. If this accompanying part appears the same way every time, then it is called the Countersubject. The Countersubject is normally written in Invertible Counterpoint, so that it can be played above or below the Answer without needing modification.

The Modulatory Section

In this section there are further entries of the Subject, often in related keys. In between these references to the Subject, there are also several small passages called Episodes. These Episodes generally consist of fragments of the Subject, or may be made up of new material altogether. Various techniques or devices are used to develop an Episode. Some typical compositional devices used in the Modulatory section are augmentation, diminution, melodic inversion, pedal points, sequences, modulation and stretto (see definitions above).

The Recapitulation, or Final Section

Here the Subject reappears, but always in the tonic key. There may be one or more entries of the Subject and Answer and quite often the entries are in Stretto (see terms above). There may be a Coda, or a formal concluding passage at the end of this section.

Italian Terms - Top 150

Here is a list of the 150 most commonly found Italian terms in music. There are many different ways to translate some of these terms, but in general the following translations are widely accepted in the music community.

If you are looking for a term that is not listed here, try an Italian dictionary or refer to the list of references on page 93.

a tempo	return to former speed
accelerando *(accel.)*	gradually becoming faster
adagietto	slow, but not as slow as 'adagio'
adagio	slowly
affettuoso	with feeling, emotion
affrettando	hurrying
agitato	hurried, with agitation
alla marcia	in strict, march tempo (usually 120 beats per minute)
allargando	gradually becoming broader
allegretto	moderately fast
allegro	lively and fast
andante	at an easy walking pace; moving, going
andantino	'small andante'; slightly faster OR slower than andante
a niente	fade to no sound
animato	with animation
appassionata	full of emotion
arco	with the bow (used after a pizz. sign)
assai	very
attacca	go on at once
ben marcato	well marked
brillante	brilliantly
bruscamente	rough, harshly
calando	getting softer and slower
cantabile	in a singing style
cantando	in a singing style

chiuso	closed (often refers to muting a horn by hand)
col legno	with the back (wooden part) of the bow
colla voce	with the voice (i.e. following the vocal line)
comodo	easily, conveniently
con amore	with love
con anima	with feeling
con brio/con spirito	with spirit
con forza	with force
con fuoco	with fire
con grazia	with grace
con moto	with movement
con sordino	with the mute
crescendo *(cresc.)*	gradually becoming louder
da capo al fine *(D.C. al fine)*	from the beginning until the word 'fine'
dal segno *(D.S.)*	from the sign
deciso	decisively
decrescendo *(decresc.)*	gradually becoming softer
deliberamente	deliberately
delicatamente/delicato	delicately
diminuendo *(dim.)*	gradually becoming softer
divisi *(div.)*	divided (split into parts)
dolce	soft and sweet, sweetly
dolcissimo	very sweetly
dolente	sadly, plaintively
doloroso	sorrowful
espressione	expression
fermata	pause
feroce	fiercely
forte *(f)*	loud
forte-piano *(fp)*	loud, then immediately soft
fortissimo *(ff)*	very loud
giocoso	gay, merry
giusto, giustamente	precise, in time

grave	slow and solemn
grazioso	gracefully
l'istesso tempo	at the same speed
lamentoso	mournfully
larghetto	rather broadly
largo, largamente	broadly
legato	smoothly, well connected (often indicated with a slur)
leggiero	lightly
lento	slowly
loco	at normal pitch (after an 8va sign)
lontano	distant, a great way off
M.M.	Maelzel's Metronome (metronome marking)
ma non troppo	but not too much
maestoso	majestically
mancando	dying away
mano destra *(M.D.)*	right hand
mano sinistra *(M.S.)*	left hand
marcato	marked
meno	less
meno mosso	less speed (slower)
mezzo forte *(mf)*	moderately loud
mezzo piano *(mp)*	moderately soft
mezzo staccato	moderately short and detached
misterioso	mysteriously
moderato	at a moderate speed
molto	very
morendo	dying away
non troppo	not too much
parlando	in recitative style
passionato	passionately
perdendosi	fading away
pesante	heavily
piacevole	pleasant, agreeable

piangendo	crying, plaintive
piangevole	plaintive
pianissimo *(pp)*	very soft
piano *(p)*	soft
più	more
piu mosso	more speed (quicker)
pizzicato *(pizz.)*	pluck the string with the finger
placido	placidly
poco	a little
poco a poco	little by little
poi	then, afterwards
portamento	slide the voice from one note to the next
prestissimo	extremely fast
presto	very fast
primo	first (part)
quasi	almost
rallentando *(rall.)*	gradually becoming slower
rinforzando *(rfz or rf)*	reinforcing the tone
riposo	restfully
risoluto	with resolution
ritardando *(rit.)*	gradually becoming slower
ritenuto *(riten. / rit.)*	immediately slower
rubato	with some freedom in the time
scherzando	playfully
sciolto	free, unconstrained
scordato	out of tune
scordatura	deliberate inexact tuning of an instrument for special effects
secondo	second (part)
semplice	simple
sempre	always
senza	without
sfogato	lightly played
sforzando *(sfz or sf)*	a strong accent

slentando	becoming slower
smorzando	dying away
sopra	over
sostenuto	sustained
sotto	under
sotto voce	softly in an undertone
spiccato	fast staccato playing on stringed instruments
staccatissimo	extremely short and detached
staccato	short and detached (indicated with a dot above or below)
strepitoso	noisy, boisterous
stringendo	pressing on faster
subito *(sub.)*	suddenly
sul	on
sul ponticello *(sul pont.)*	bow on or near the bridge
sul tasto	bow on or near the finger board
tanto	so much
tempo	speed
tempo commodo	at a comfortable speed
tempo giusto	at a consistent speed
teneramente	tenderly
tenuto *(ten.)*	held
tranquillo	calmly
tre corde *(T.C.)* **or tutte le corde**	(three strings) release the soft pedal on the piano
tremolo	bowing very rapidly to produce a shimmering or wavering effect
tutti	passage for the entire ensemble or orchestra without a soloist
una corda *(U.C.)*	(one string) with the soft pedal on the piano
vivace	lively and spirited
vivo	lively and spirited

French Terms - Top 50

French terms are less common than Italian terms, but in French music (such as that of Ravel or Debussy) many of the terms indicating expression and mood are in French, while there may also be a few Italian markings.

French music is well known for its elongated instructions such as 'rythme doit avoir la valeur sonore d'un fond de paysage triste et glacé' or 'comme un echo de la phrase entendue précédemment'. For sentences such as these, you'll need to consult a French dictionary!

Here is a list of the 50 most commonly found terms in French music. If you are looking for a term that is not listed here, try a French dictionary or refer to the list of references on page 93.

à plein son	a full sound
animé	lively, animated
appuyé	sustained, leaned on
au dessous du mouvement	in a slower tempo
au mouvt/au mouvement	a tempo
avec	with
avec sourdine	muted
beaucoup	a lot, much
cédez	go slower
doucement	softly, sweetly
doux	sweet
égal	equal
en chantant	in a singing style
en diminuant	getting softer
en rallentissant	getting slower
en retardant	getting slower
gracieux	graciously
grave	slow, dignified
jouissance (avec)	joyously
jusqu'à la fin	until the end

laissez vibrer	allow to resonate, do not dampen
léger	light
légèrement	lightly
lent	slow
lointain	distant
lourd	heavy
main droite (*M.D.*)	right hand
main gauche (*M.G.*)	left hand
majestueux	majestically
marqué	marked
modéré	moderately
moins	less
moins vif	less lively
plus	more
plus lent	more slowly
pressez	move on, accelerate
puissant	powerfully
retenu	hold back the tempo
sans	without
sans lourdeur	without heaviness
sans rigueur	without rigour
sec	dry
soutenu	sustained
suivez	follow
très	very
très vif	very lively
un peu	a little
un peu en dehors	a little stressed
vif	vivacious

German Terms - Top 40

German terms are far less common than Italian terms. Occasionally Beethoven or Schubert notated a tempo or expression marking in German, but the majority were in Italian.

Here is a list of the 40 most commonly found German terms in music. There are many different ways to translate some of these terms, but in general these translations are widely accepted in the music community. Please also note that the German symbol 'ß' is sometimes equated to the English 'ss' in spelling.

If you are looking for a term that is not listed here, try a German dictionary or refer to the list of references on page 93.

allmählich	gradually
bewegt	moving, agitated
breiter werdend	becoming broader
erstes Zeitmaß (Zeitmass)	original tempo
etwas breiter	somewhat more broadly
etwas lebhafter	somewhat faster
gedämpft	muted
geschwind	swiftly
gestopft	stopped
gestützt	sustained
halb laut	moderately loud
halb leise	moderately soft
immer	continuing onwards, always
langsam	slowly
langsamer werdend	getting slower
laut	strong/loud
lebhaft(er)	(more) lively
leise	soft
mäßig (mässig)	at a moderate speed
mit Dämpfer	with the mute
mit Kraft	with force, strong

nachlassend	becoming softer, diminishing
nicht	not
ohne	without
ohne Dämpfer	without mute
rasch	quick, swift
ruhig	calm
sanft	sweet, soft
schnell	fast
sehr	very
träumerisch	dreamily
traurig	sad
verlöschend	dying away
verzögert	slower
volles Zeitmaß (Zeitmass)	full tempo
wie vorher	as before
wieder	again
mit Geist	with spirit
Zeitmaß (Zeitmass)	tempo
zurückgehalten	held back

The Main Periods in Music History

Music history is usually divided into 'periods'. The main periods are:

★ Renaissance (Pre-Baroque)

★ Baroque

★ Classical

★ Romantic

★ Impressionist

★ Modern/20th and 21st Century (1900 - present)

The following pages contain information about each of these periods. There is a detailed description of the style, history and evolution of each period, as well as a table showing the main features of the music of that period.

You need to have some knowledge of the stylistic characteristics of these periods as well as how they relate to the pieces you are playing and studying. For example, if you are playing a piece by Debussy, you will need to know general information about the Impressionist period, but more importantly which of the main stylistic features of the Impressionist period appear in your piece.

 For more detailed information on historical events surrounding these musical periods, go to **www.blitzbooks.com**

Pre-Baroque Music

MUSIC BEFORE 800 A.D.

Our knowledge about music of ancient civilisations (Egyptians, Greeks, Romans, etc.) is quite limited. Although we have some idea of the instruments, scales and modes used by the ancient Greeks, we know much more about music from the Christian Era onwards (from about 200 A.D.). Religious (sacred) music during this period consisted mainly of Plainsong or Gregorian Chant (see page 20), while non-religious (secular) music consisted of folk songs. Both sacred and secular music were 'monodic', consisting of a single melodic line without accompaniment, harmony or counterpoint.

POLYPHONY BEGINS (see page 51)

From about 800 A.D. it became quite popular to sing Plainsong or Gregorian Chant in two parts, a perfect 5th or perfect 4th apart. This style was called 'Organum' and was quite established by the 13th century. Organum then began to employ melodic and rhythmic imitation, along with much greater freedom in the rhythmic and harmonic language used. Music was steadily becoming more complex and over the next few centuries this evolved into Polyphony (see Polyphonic, page 51).

THE RENAISSANCE: 1400-1600

The Renaissance period was a very exciting time to live in. There was a surge of interest in the sciences, exploration and the arts. Today we still place great value on works by Renaissance artists such as Leonardo da Vinci and Michelangelo.

The Renaissance period was also a turning point for music. Often called the 'Golden Age of Polyphony', Renaissance music is marked by a complex and lush interweaving of melodic lines in vocal as well as instrumental composition. Secular music blossomed alongside sacred music, and imitation was increasingly combined with polyphonic techniques for composition of all types of music. While up until then vocal composition had been the main focus, instrumental music was steadily gaining popularity and composers enjoyed using forms such as variations, fantasies, toccatas and dances. With the invention of the printing press, sheet music became widely available.

Giovanni Palestrina was one of the most polished and prolific composers of the Renaissance. His flowing counterpoint style is still taught as part of advanced theory courses to this day.

The Baroque Period (c.1600-1750)

Although the French word Baroque can be literally translated as 'bizarre', it is rarely interpreted this way in relation to music. Baroque is a term originally used to describe the ornate architecture of the same period.

Many important musical developments took place during the Baroque period. For the first time, instrumental music became as important as choral music, while keyboard music for the harpsichord and pipe organ was especially popular. The origins of the modern orchestra can be found in this period, along with the earliest forms of opera, the concerto, sonata, and modern cantata. Works for instruments included Suites, Partitas, Fugues and Sonatas for various combinations of instruments. Music for orchestra included Sinfonias and Concertos, especially the Concerto Grosso (see Chapter 2 beginning on page 10 for definitions of all of these titles).

A most important feature of the Baroque period is the way composers continued to develop and extend the use of polyphony: two or more independent parts combining to make a complex tapestry of sound, following all the intricate rules of counterpoint writing. Imitation was another feature of the Baroque period which was almost inseparable from polyphony - the interweaving melodies imitating each other so cleverly that no single voice could be identified as taking the leading role. Some Baroque composers, like Handel, also used a lighter-textured homophonic style, in which one main melody was supported by a chordal accompaniment.

Baroque music is balanced, controlled and often mathematical in its precision. The structure is always formal and tight while counterpoint is ever-present. J.S. Bach, the greatest composer of the Baroque period, worked within these formal constraints to compose music of remarkable majesty, creativity and richness.

For the Baroque performer, the challenge of bringing out the independence as well as the imitative qualities of each voice requires a range of articulations and dynamic contrasts. There are many conventions and traditions when it comes to Baroque articulation and many different schools of thought regarding the use of modern instruments for this music. (For example, harpsichords were incapable of subtle dynamics; should we then not use dynamics when playing Bach's music on a modern piano?) It is up to the individual performer to decide on the best interpretation after careful thought and analysis.

MAIN CHARACTERISTICS OF BAROQUE MUSIC	
Melody	Single motif dominates the whole composition; counterpoint and imitation used throughout; much use of ornamentation and embellishment; sequences and inversions used to develop and modify the melody.
Harmony	Old church modes abandoned; modern harmonic system adopted based upon the major and minor scales; new tuning systems such as Equal Temperament introduced for keyboard instruments; modulations to very closely related keys.
Rhythm / Tempo	Strong constant rhythmic pulse; repetition frequently used.
Dynamics	'Terrace' or 'block' dynamics, i.e. blocks of sound rather than subtle crescendos and diminuendos.
Articulation	Varied articulations to bring out different contrapuntal features. Modern performers should use little or no sustain pedal; articulation always clear and succinct.
Form / Structure	Short dance movements in Binary form were the most popular among composers; 'Concerto Grosso' form dominates orchestral music. The most complex form for keyboard music was the Fugue.
Texture	Polyphonic or multi-stranded.
Interpretation	The 'Doctrine of Affects' was an important theory of the time. It dictated that music should evoke only one mood for the whole piece.

MAIN BAROQUE COMPOSERS	
Germany	J.S. Bach, Handel, Pachelbel, Buxtehude, Telemann
Italy	Monteverdi, A. Scarlatti, D. Scarlatti, A. Corelli, Vivaldi, Tartini
France	Lully, Couperin, Rameau
England	Purcell

The Classical Period (c.1750-1825)

←───→

EARLY CLASSICAL OR PRE-CLASSICAL

Composers such as Couperin, C.P.E. Bach and J.C. Bach were the predecessors of the Classical period. These composers represented a style called Rococo or Style Galante, an elaborate yet light style which contrasted with the heavier and more contrapuntal Baroque style. The two most significant Classical composers, Mozart and Haydn, were greatly influenced by the Rococo style.

CLASSICAL MUSIC

Classical music shares some characteristics with the values of the ancient Greeks, who pursued the ideals of beauty, clarity, and proportion. Classical composers were most concerned with balance, structure and precision in their compositions.

The Classical period is often referred to as the Viennese Classical Period or the First Viennese School because the main classical composers were centred in Vienna. These composers established the standard principles of Sonata form, which have greatly influenced instrumental composition to the present day.

Although the Classical period is comparatively shorter than other periods, many changes took place in this time. The size and structure of the modern orchestra was established and the older style of 'opera seria' gave way to the lighter, more comic 'opera buffa' style exemplified by Mozart works in the genre. Keyboard instruments evolved; the forte-piano gradually took over from the harpsichord as the main keyboard instrument of the Classical period. The use of polyphony and counterpoint gave way to a more homophonic style, in which the melodic line featured in one part, while the other parts provided an accompaniment, often in the form of a light and buoyant Alberti bass (see page 46).

There was a new focus on dynamics; composers used the full spectrum of tonal shading to breathe life and drama into the musical interpretation of a piece. The dynamic capabilities of the forte-piano encouraged this new approach, as did the influence of the 'Mannheim School' in the 18th century, a movement which placed much importance on extended crescendos and decrescendos and precise dynamics in orchestral playing.

The Classical style demands elegance and pristine clarity in performance, with perfectly proportioned dynamics and phrasing. To play in convincing period style, the Classical performer needs to observe the tiniest details of phrasing and articulation.

This sparkling style can seem deceptively simple but there is often much emotional depth and imagination just under the surface.

MAIN CHARACTERISTICS OF CLASSICAL MUSIC	
Melody	Passage work with subdued accompaniment; sequences, repetition and ornamentation not as frequent as in Baroque music; more use of the appoggiatura and gradual decline of the mordent.
Harmony	Harmony based on primary triads (I, IV and V); modulations to closely related keys.
Rhythm / Tempo	Strong pulse; always steady and controlled; few changes of tempo within one movement.
Dynamics	Much broader dynamic range, although always balanced and never excessive in any way. Frequent use of crescendos and diminuendos.
Phrasing	Regular and balanced phrases; frequent use of the two-note phrase (the second note generally shorter and lighter).
Articulation	More use of legato; sparse use of keyboard pedal. Use of subtle articulation markings (staccatissimo, mezzo-staccato, tenuto) to create a variety of refined textures.
Form / Structure	Formal structure (especially Sonata form) considered of major importance.
Texture	Homophonic rather than polyphonic, the melody assigned to just one part.
Interpretation	Buoyant playing required to create a sparkling, elegant, and polished style; fast passages to sound easy and unlaboured.

MAIN CLASSICAL COMPOSERS	
Italy	Clementi
Germany / Austria	Mozart, Haydn, early Beethoven, early Schubert

The Romantic Period (c.1825-1920)

←——————————————————————→

EARLY ROMANTIC (c.1825–c.1860); LATE ROMANTIC (c.1860–c.1920)

The term 'Romantic' applies to many aspects of culture during the 19th century. It was the age of the individual, of the common man becoming important, and this spirit now pervaded literature and art as well as music. Originality and the creative ego were prized qualities.

The Romantic period has often been referred to as the 'golden age of the virtuoso'. Ferociously difficult pieces were performed on pianos that had a wider range of notes, were stronger and louder, and which could fill a concert hall with sound.

In sharp contrast to the Classical period, the emotional range of Romantic music was much wider. Romantic composers were more interested in shouting their personal triumphs and expressing their innermost feelings than adhering to formal structure. A single piece of music might suddenly swing from profound inner reflection to agitated impatience and explosive fury. This type of composition became far more important than, for example, rigidly following the rules of Sonata form.

The elements of music – melody, rhythm, harmony - all reflected the new focus on emotional expression. Melodies were far more lyrical, with longer, sweeping phrasing that more effectively expressed the warmth of personal feeling. There was also much use of chromaticism. Rubato became an important performance feature of the Romantic period, allowing the performer to let the tempo breathe more flexibly with the dramatic content. At times, cross-rhythms were also introduced by the Romantic composer to enhance the sense of complex feeling or drama.

The tonal language was now far more daring too, with sudden modulations and increasing use of unrelated keys. Harmonies were often rich and dark, involving pointed dissonances to suggest inner turmoil, anguish and tension.

Romantic composers enjoyed writing music based on historical tales or legends, often of a tragic or despairing nature. Shakespeare's plays were used as the subject of many instrumental and vocal compositions, and composers also took inspiration from the poetry of the time, resulting in the German 'lied' or art song (see page 21 and page 11). There was new interest in nationalistic music and folk song (e.g. Dvořák's Slavonic Dances, Liszt's Hungarian Rhapsodies).

The Romantic era was a time of musical extremes, from the grandiose, large-scale operas of Verdi and Wagner, to the miniature character sketches of Chopin, Schumann and Mendelssohn. Some of the new shorter forms which became regular features of the Romantic repertoire were the Nocturne, Prelude, Waltz, Romance, Study, Lied, Ballade, Intermezzo and Songs Without Words. (Definitions can be found on page 10.)

MAIN CHARACTERISTICS OF ROMANTIC MUSIC	
Melody	Lyrical and deeply expressive, often featuring chromaticism.
Harmony	Movement away from the restrictions of the Classical era; inclusion of chromaticism and dissonances; modulations to unrelated keys.
Rhythm / Tempo	Tempo changes more frequent, rubato often employed.
Dynamics	Sudden and confronting dynamic changes often used to express the intensity of the composer's emotions.
Phrasing	Longer, often irregular phrases.
Articulation	Predominantly legato and flowing, with much use of the pedal.
Form / Structure	Structure and form far less important than the emotional content. Sonata form less common; shorter pieces (often composed in collections) more popular.
Texture	Dense but almost always homophonic texture; focus on harmony and melody, almost no polyphony.
Interpretation	Emotional and expressive playing required. Movement away from the 'polite' performances of the preceding Classical era.

MAIN ROMANTIC COMPOSERS	
Germany	Wagner, Schumann, Mendelssohn, Brahms, late Schubert, late Beethoven
Italy	Puccini, Verdi, Paganini
Russia	Tchaikovsky, Rachmaninov
Other	Berlioz (France), Saint-Saëns (France), Chopin (Poland), Liszt (Hungary)

The Impressionist Period (c.1890-1920)

←—————————————————————————————→

'Impressionism' was a term first used from about 1870 to describe the style of a group of French painters who used blurred outlines and the effects of light to convey an 'impression' of a scene rather than a sharply defined representation. The famous Impressionist painter Monet called his painting of a sunrise at sea 'une impression' while Manet, in an exhibition catalogue, stated his desire to create his own 'impression' of the subject matter. From then on the term was widely used.

At about the same time, a small group of like-minded French musicians also defined themselves as Impressionists. These musicians were inspired by both the Impressionist painters and the French 'Symbolist' poets of the period. The Symbolists aimed at expressing their own personal feelings and impressions about a certain subject, rather than the literal depiction of the subject in the poem.

The Impressionist musicians followed this philosophy of evoking personal feelings and emotions through their music. While much of the music from the preceding Romantic period set out to tell a specific story or describe a particular emotion, Impressionist music was far more vague and slippery. As a reaction against the Romantic period (especially the music of Wagner), strong emotions were now deliberately avoided.

The focus for Impressionist composers was simply the mood and atmosphere aroused by a subject, without the tension and emphatic emotions expressed by previous Romantics. Debussy was so concerned that his music should create a uniquely personal impression on the performer that many of the descriptive titles of his pieces actually appear at the end of the music rather than at the start (for example in his Preludes, Books 1 and 2).

Impressionists used a variety of unconventional techniques to achieve delicate and ethereal effects. Traditional rules of harmony were not followed; 5ths, 8ves and groups of triads moved freely in parallel motion, with pedalling deliberately aimed at smudging and overlapping the harmonies. Unconventional scale patterns were used, while underlying harmonies were often ambiguous and unresolved, robbing the piece of a tonal centre and clear harmonic direction. There were 'splashes' of sound, with misty, shadowy, velvety effects built up through layered textures. Small atmospheric pieces such as preludes and nocturnes were favoured over long sonatas and concertos.

MAIN CHARACTERISTICS OF IMPRESSIONIST MUSIC	
Melody	Long, flowing phrases; use of unusual scales (e.g. whole tone, pentatonic, modes); melodic line not always as important as the underlying mood or atmosphere.
Harmony	Tonality increasingly vague and ambiguous; chords often extended with 6ths, 7ths, 9ths, 11ths etc.; dissonances are unprepared and unresolved; harmonies often smudged and blurred by sustain pedal; extended pedal notes or ostinati bass with changing harmonies.
Rhythm / Tempo	Use of free and complex rhythms; use of cross-rhythms and syncopation; time signature changes mid-piece; frequent changes of tempo.
Dynamics	Full range of dynamics employed but without the dramatic changes of the Romantic period.
Articulation	Little use of accents so as to maximise the flow of the music; much use of sustaining pedal to smudge harmonies and create misty atmospheres.
Form / Structure	Short atmospheric pieces favoured over long sonatas or concertos.
Texture	Often multi-layered; little use of imitation; much use of ethereal, vapoury textures.
Interpretation	Delicacy and subtlety almost always a priority; avoidance of strong emotional tension; creation of atmospheres and silky textures.

MAIN IMPRESSIONIST COMPOSERS	
France	Claude Debussy, Maurice Ravel, Erik Satie, Paul Dukas
England	Frederick Delius
Russia	Alexander Scriabin
USA	Charles Griffes

The Modern Period (c.1900-present)

←——————————————————————————————→

Music of the Modern period is often referred to as '20th-century' music, even though we are well into the 21st century!

Since the early 1900s, music has been going through major changes. There was initially a reaction against both the German Romantic tradition and the French Impressionist movement. In the quest to create a new language and new forms, composers have developed music that is edgy, experimental and radically different to that of past centuries.

There are many different styles within the Modern period, as composers have followed their desire to be individual:

★ Expressionism

★ Neo-Classicism

★ Musique Concrète/Electroacoustic Music

★ Neo-Primitivism

★ Serialism

★ Nationalism

★ Indeterminate/Chance Music/Aleatoric Music

★ Neo-Romanticism/Post Romanticism

★ Electronic Music

★ Minimalism

 There are brief definitions of some of these styles in Chapter 3 (from page 41), but you can go to **www.blitzbooks.com** for detailed information (including dates and the main composers of each style) on all of the Modern styles listed above.

MAIN CHARACTERISTICS OF THE MODERN ERA	
Melody	Angular melodies with sharp contours, often created quite artificially and randomly. Absence of lyrical melodies, emotionally detached.
Harmony	Bi-tonal, often atonal with much use of dissonances and modal harmony (Ionian, Dorian, Phrygian, etc.). Tonal centre often ambiguous.
Rhythm / Tempo	Sharp, very rhythmic, with much syncopation and energy. Unpredictable changes of time signature, complex rhythms and cross-rhythms used.
Dynamics	A wide variety of approaches but often loud and confronting.
Articulation	Also varied, but often crisp and dry. Sparse use of pedal, sometimes other effects employed such as a 'prepared' piano which has foreign objects fixed to the strings to create strange articulation effects
Form	No restrictions.
Texture	Anything from sparse to dense, depending on the mood of the composer/performer.
Interpretation	Much more licence given to the performer; music often reflecting the anxieties, fears, pressures and cynicism of contemporary life.

MAIN COMPOSERS OF THE MODERN ERA	
Germany	Paul Hindemith, Karlheinz Stockhausen, Richard Strauss
Austria	Alban Berg, Anton Webern, Arnold Schoenberg
America	Aaron Copland, John Cage, George Gershwin, Samuel Barber, Steve Reich, Philip Glass, John Adams
Russia	Igor Stravinsky, Sergei Prokofiev
France	Pierre Boulez, Francis Poulenc, Georges Auric
Italy	Alfredo Casella, Luciano Berio, Gian Francesco Malipiero
Hungary	Béla Bartók
England	Gustav Holst, Ralph Vaughan Williams, Benjamin Britten
Poland	Krzysztof Penderecki, Henryk Górecki
Estonia	Arvo Pärt

Key Relationships

A **modulation** is a change of key. A piece that has changed key will usually have at least two or three bars of music in that key before it changes again. The music will often contain many accidentals: this means the composer has decided to change key without changing the key signature.

Occasionally the change of key is very short (maybe only one bar) - this is sometimes referred to as a **tonicisation**.

When an examiner asks you about the modulations in your exam pieces, it's really good if you can explain the **relationship** of the new key to the old key.

Pieces will usually modulate to a 'related' key. The closest relative is the one with the same key signature (i.e. the relative major or relative minor) or a key signature only one sharp or one flat away from its own. Here is an example of the tonic key 'family tree' of C major:

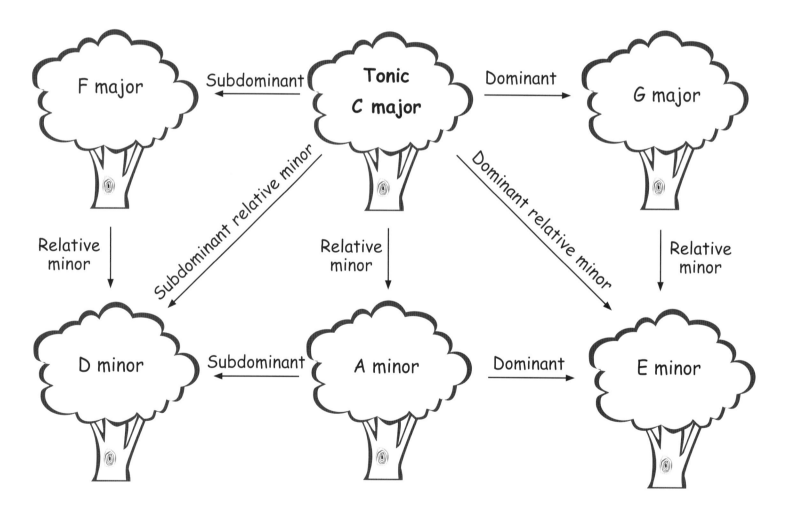

As you can see from the diagram above, a piece in C major is most likely to modulate to any one of its closest relatives: its relative minor key, the dominant and subdominant keys and/ or their relative minors.

Pieces in minor keys have the same family tree but would modulate to the relative **major** or to the dominant **minor** or subdominant **minor**. (N.B. Even though the dominant chord in a minor key is a major chord, the dominant key of a minor key is always minor.)

Knowing the closest relatives of any key helps a lot when you are trying to work out the modulations in your exam pieces. Remember to identify the **relationship** of the new key to the tonic key (e.g. dominant, subdominant).

OTHER KEY RELATIONSHIPS

Keys that are two flats or two sharps away from the tonic key signature are slightly more distant relatives. For example, a modulation from B flat major (two flats) to A flat major (four flats) is basically going to the subdominant key of the subdominant key!

Keys that are three sharps or three flats away are extremely distant **unless the piece is changing tonality**, in which case it is said to be modulating to the 'tonic major' or 'tonic minor' and is considered to be quite well related! For example:

E flat major (three flats) to E flat minor (six flats)

B minor (two sharps) to B major (five sharps)

G major (one sharp) to G minor (two flats)

D minor (one flat) to D major (two sharps)

Did you notice that the last two modulations listed above change from a sharp key to a flat key and vice versa? This happens all the time in music and does not necessarily mean the two keys are unrelated!

A modulation to a key four or more sharps or flats away is pretty much considered to be an 'unrelated' key. The composer Franz Schubert was famous for the unrelated modulations in his works.

You will see on page 91 there is an opportunity to write down the tonic keys of your exam pieces, and list the main modulations and key relationships.

 For a thorough understanding of key relationships, download free worksheets and the 'Key Signature Number Line' from **www.blitzbooks.com**

The Seven Modes

Modes are scales which can best be understood if we start by looking at the scale of C major. If we decided to play C major beginning and ending on the second note of the scale (i.e. from D to D, without any sharps or flats), then we would have just played the Dorian mode on D. The Dorian mode can actually be played starting on any note, as long as it contains the same sequence of tones and semitones found when playing only 'white' notes from D to D.

Each mode has a very distinctive sound due to its pattern of tones and semitones. The names of the seven surviving 'church' modes are based on ancient Greek regions and tribes:

Ionian (same as the major scale, C to C)

Dorian (D-D)

Phrygian (E-E)

Lydian (F-F)

Mixolydian (G-G)

Aeolian (same as the natural minor scale, A-A)

Locrian (B-B)

Just as major and minor scales can begin on any tonic, the modes can also be transposed to begin on any note. So a piece in the Mixolydian mode may begin on F and would feature B flat and E flat (known as F Mixolydian).

A great way to remember the order of the modes is to use a 'mnemonic' - a sentence in which each word begins with the first letter of the mode. Here are some cool mnemonics:

I Don't Play Like Mozart And Liszt

I Don't Particularly Like Modes A Lot

I Don't Play Loud Music After Lunch

I Don't Play Like My Aunt Lucy

Modes are often used by jazz musicians because certain modes sound really good over various jazz chords. The modes give musicians the ingredients from which to make up melodies, or to improvise.

Composers

On the following seven pages, you will find information on the 150 most-featured composers in exam syllabuses, as well as most of the main composers in music history. If you can't find the composer you're looking for, it's not due to lack of fame or talent, but simply due to the fact that your composer may not have many pieces on exam lists.

The information is presented in table format and the composers are listed in alphabetical order. For each composer you will find:

★ Birth and death dates (correct at the time of publishing this book)

★ Country of birth

★ Period of composition (in this table we have categorised anyone after 1900 as 'Modern')

★ Main works

★ Contemporaries (other composers living/working at the same time)

This table is only a little taste of the wealth of information available about any composer. However, you can put together a very intelligent sounding paragraph just from the basic information in the table! For example, here is the 'row' about Bach:

COMPOSER	DATES	BIRTH-PLACE	PERIOD	MAJOR WORKS	CONTEM-PORARIES
Bach, Johann Sebastian (J.S.)	1685 - 1750	Germany	Baroque	Keyboard: *The Well-Tempered Clavier, French Suites, English Suites*; 200 Cantatas; *Christmas Oratorio*; Organ: *Toccata and Fugue in D minor*	Handel, Purcell

Now here is an example of how you would put this information together for an exam:

"Bach was born in Germany in 1685. He was a composer of the Baroque period. He wrote many famous works including The Well-Tempered Clavier, 200 Cantatas, the Christmas Oratorio and 'Toccata and Fugue in D minor' for the organ. Other composers that lived during this time were Handel and Purcell. Bach died in 1750."

Not bad, eh? However, if you are attempting **Grade 7 or 8 or higher**, you will need to know much more about your composers than just the information listed in the table. The easiest and probably best resource for this is the internet, but check out the list of suggested references on page 93.

COMPOSER	DATES	BIRTH-PLACE	PERIOD	MAJOR WORKS	CONTEM-PORARIES
Agay, Denes	1911 - 2007	Hungary	Modern	Orchestral and band works, solo songs, woodwind music, piano pieces: *Blue Waltz*	Alexander, Rollin
Albéniz, Isaac	1860 - 1909	Spain	Late Romantic	Operas: *Henry Clifford*; operettas, piano works: *Suite Iberia*; orchestral pieces: *Catalonia*	Fauré, Granados
Alexander, Dennis	1947 -	United States	Modern	Works for students, mainly for piano: *A Splash of Colour* Bks 1 and 2, *24 Character Preludes*	Bastien, Rollin
Alkan, Charles	1813 - 1888	France	Romantic	Many piano pieces: *Grande Sonate*, *Les Quatre Âges*, *Sonatine*, 12 Etudes Op. 39	Liszt, Schumann
Arnold, Malcolm	1921 - 2006	England	Modern	Symphonies: *Toy Symphony*, *Concerto for Guitar* Op. 67; piano pieces: *Children's Suite*	Britten, Crosse
Bach, Carl Philipp Emanuel	1714 - 1788	Germany	Pre - Classical	Over 200 keyboard sonatas, 50 concertos, violin sonatas, oratorios, 22 passions, other large vocal works: *Magnificat*	Benda, Homilius
Bach, Johann Sebastian (J.S.)	1685 - 1750	Germany	Baroque	Keyboard: *The Well-Tempered Clavier, French Suites, English Suites*; passions, 200 Cantatas, *Christmas Oratorio*, Organ: *Toccata and Fugue in D minor*	Handel, Purcell
Bailey, Kerin	1949 -	Australia	Modern	Piano works: *Jazzin' Around* series, *Jazz Incorporated* series	Edwards, Westlake
Barratt, Carol	1945 -	England	Modern	Variety of works for students: *Bravo;* many songs, piano albums: *Play it Again Chester*	Wedgwood, Norton
Bartók, Béla	1881 - 1945	Hungary	Modern	Folk dances, ballets: *The Miraculous Mandarin*; opera: *Bluebeard's Castle*; Orchestra: *Concerto for Orchestra*	Kodály, Stravinsky
Bastien, James	1934 - 2005	United States	Modern	Variety of educational material for students: *Pop Piano Styles, Favorite Classic Melodies*	Wedgwood, Alexander
Beethoven, Ludwig van	1770 - 1827	Germany	Classical/ Romantic	Nine symphonies, 32 piano sonatas: *Waldstein, Pathetique, Moonlight*, five piano concertos: *Emperor*	Haydn, Weber
Benjamin, Arthur	1893 - 1960	Australia	Modern	Piano works: *Jamaican Rumba*; harmonica concerto; operas: *A Tale of Two Cities*	Hyde, Britten
Berens, Hermann	1826 - 1880	Germany	Romantic	Piano works: *Melodious Exercises* Op. 62, *The Music Box, 20 Children's Studies* Op. 79	Gurlitt, Liszt
Berkeley, Lennox	1903 - 1989	England	Modern	Four symphonies; operas: *A Dinner Engagement;* piano pieces: *Six Preludes*	Tippet, Britten
Bertini, Henri	1798 - 1876	England	Romantic	500 etudes, nonets, sextets, fantasias, rondos, three symphonies for piano and orchestra	Hummel, Kalkbrenner
Boccherini, Luigi	1743 - 1803	Italy	Classical	30 symphonies, 91 string quartets, 154 quintets, cello concertos, trios	Haydn, Cimarosa
Boehm, Theobald	1794 - 1881	Germany	Romantic	Many flute pieces: *Fantasie on a Theme of Schubert, Flute Concerto No. 1 in G*	Spohr, Bertini
Bonsor, Brian	1926 - 2011	Scotland	Modern	Various piano pieces, mainly for students: *Wistful Prelude, Girl on a Cat-walk, Dreamy*	Urquhart-Jones, Brubeck
Boyd, Anne	1946 -	Australia	Modern	Orchestra: *Black Sun*; vocal: *Summer Nights*; piano: *The Book of Bells*	Westlake, Edwards
Bozza, Eugène	1905 - 1991	France	Modern	Ballets: *Lille, Jeux de Plage*; violin concerto; chamber works: *Ricercare*	Messiaen, Jolivet
Brahms, Johannes	1833 - 1897	Germany	Romantic	Symphonies, concertos, *A German Requiem*, Hungarian Dances, song cycles, piano sonatas, intermezzos	Liszt, Schumann
Brandman, Margaret	1951 -	Australia	Modern	Saxophone quartet, string orchestra: *Undulations*; voice: *Songs of Love and Despair*; piano: *Sonorities*, educational albums	Edwards, Westlake
Bridge, Frank	1879 - 1941	England	Late Rom/ Modern	*Phantasie Piano Quartet in F minor*; orchestra: *Dance Rhapsody, The Sea*; piano sonata	Vaughan Williams, Bax

COMPOSER	DATES	BIRTH-PLACE	PERIOD	MAJOR WORKS	CONTEM-PORARIES
Britten, Benjamin	1913 - 1976	England	Modern	Operas: *Peter Grimes, Death in Venice*; orchestral works, vocal works, chamber and solo works	Walton, Tippett
Brubeck, Dave	1920 - 2012	United States	Modern	Jazz combos: *Dialogues, Summersong;* many piano solos: *Blue Rondo a la Turk*	Shearing, Solal
Brumby, Colin	1933 -	Australia	Modern	Ballets: *Masques, Hippolytus;* opera: *La Donna;* voice: three Pastorals; orchestra: oboe concerto	Sitsky, Williamson
Burgmüller, Johann F.	1806 - 1874	Germany	Romantic	Ballet: *La Péri;* piano studies: Op. 100, orchestral music for ballet '*Giselle*'	Liszt, Schumann
Busoni, Ferruccio B.	1866 - 1924	Italy	Late Romantic	Operas: *Turandot, Doktor Faust, Arlecchino,* violin concerto; orchestra: *Berceuse Élégiaque*	Mahler, Sibelius
Carr, Edwin	1926 - 2003	New Zealand	Modern	Orchestra: *Aubade;* ballet: *Electra;* choral: *Easter Cantata, Waikato Song*	Chua, Kats - Chernin
Carter-Varney, Glennis	1938 -	Australia	Modern	Piano albums: *Kool Jazzy Tunes;* piano solos: *Summer Dreaming, Sonic Fantasy, Shades of Blue*	Brandman, Bailey
Chaminade, Cécile	1857 - 1944	France	Late Romantic	Opéra-comique, *Les Amazones* for chorus and orchestra, *Concertstück* for piano and orchestra	Debussy, Mahler
Chopin, Frédéric	1810 - 1849	Poland	Romantic	Piano: *Preludes* Op. 28, Nocturnes, Etudes: Op. 10 and Op. 25, Ballades: Op. 23; *Fantasie Impromptu*	Liszt, Schumann
Chua, Sonny	1967 -	Malaysia	Modern	Various piano works: *Midnight Snack, Astral Air, Death by Pasta;* album: *Red Hot Rhapsodies*	Kats-Chernin, Norton
Cimarosa, Domenico	1749 - 1801	Italy	Classical	Operas: *Le Stravaganze del Conte, Penelope;* keyboard: 30 sonatas, piano concertos, choral works: *Requiem*	Boccherini, Haydn
Clementi, Muzio	1752 - 1832	Italy	Classical	Many keyboard studies: *Gradus ad Parnassum* Op. 44; over 60 keyboard sonatas, sonatinas, symphonies	Cramer, Mozart
Copland, Aaron	1900 - 1990	United States	Modern	Ballets: *Appalachian Spring;* orchestra: *Dance Symphony, Fanfare for the Common Man*	Ives, Milhaud
Corelli, Arcangelo	1653 - 1713	Italy	Baroque	*Sonatas da Camera a Tre; Christmas Concerto* Op. 8 for strings and continuo, concerto grossi	Scarlatti, Purcell
Couperin, Francois	1668 - 1773	France	Baroque	Over 230 harpsichord pieces: *Pieces de Clavecin,* 42 organ pieces, chamber music: *Les Nations*	Corelli, Rameau
Czerny, Carl	1791 - 1857	Austria	Classical	Piano studies: *Left Hand Etudes* Op. 718; sonatas: *Sonata Sentimentale* Op. 10; over 1000 compositions	Beethoven, Hummel
Daquin, Louis Claude	1694 - 1772	France	Baroque	Harpsichord pieces: *The Cuckoo, Nouveau Livre de Noëls;* organ pieces	Rameau, Couperin
Debussy, Claude	1862 - 1918	France	Impres-sionist	Orchestra: *Prélude à l'Après-midi d'un Faune;* piano: *Images, Iberia;* operas: *Pelléas et Mélisande*	Satie, Ravel
Delius, Frederick	1862 - 1934	England	Late Romantic	Orchestra: *Brigg Fair, In a Summer Garden, North Country Sketches;* concertos, songs	Ravel, Elgar
Diabelli, Anton	1781 - 1858	Austria	Romantic	Six masses, waltz, pieces for guitar: five Viennese Dances, operetta: *Adam in der Klemme*	Czerny, Schubert
Doppler, Franz Albert	1821 - 1883	Ukraine	Romantic	Piano: *Pásztor Hangok, Impromptu;* orchestra: *Hungarian Overture;* ballads, songs	Liszt, Schumann
Dussek, Johann	1760 - 1812	Czecho-slovakia	Classical/Romantic	*Military Concerto* Op. 40; much chamber music: *Notturno Concertante;* piano: *Farewell Sonata*	Haydn, Schubert
Duvernoy, Victor	1842 - 1907	France	Romantic	Symphonic poem: *La Tempête;* chamber music, piano: *School of Mechanism* Op. 120, flute pieces	Dvořák, Debussy
Dvořák, Antonín	1841 - 1904	Czecho-slovakia	Late Romantic	Cello concerto, string quartets, nine symphonies, *The Noonday Witch:* piano: *Slavonic Dances*	Smetana, Wagner

COMPOSER	DATES	BIRTH-PLACE	PERIOD	MAJOR WORKS	CONTEM-PORARIES
Edwards, Ross	1942 -	Australia	Modern	Several film scores, children's music, five symphonies, vocal music, oboe concerto	Vine, Sculthorpe
Elgar, Sir Edward (William)	1857 - 1934	England	Romantic	Symphonies, concertos: *Cello Concerto*; oratorios, orchestral works: *Variations on an Original Theme* (Enigma), *Pomp and Circumstance March No. 4*; chamber and solo works	Parry, Stanford
Evans, Bill	1929 - 1980	United States	Modern	Many jazz piano solos: *Waltz for Debby, Comrade Conrad, Time Rememebered, Peace Piece*	Brubeck, Peterson
Falla, Manuel de	1876 - 1946	Spain	Late Romantic	Piano: *Pièces Espagnoles*; concerto: *Nights in the Garden of Spain*; opera: *La Vida Breve*	Ravel, Arbos
Fauré, Gabriel	1845 - 1924	France	Late Romantic	Choral: *Requiem*; piano impromptus, songs: La *Chanson d'Ève*; orchestral suite: *Pelléas et Mélisande*	Saint-Saëns, Debussy
Franck, César	1822 - 1890	France	Romantic	Organ: *Six Pièces pour Grand Orgue, Mass for Three Voices*; orchestra: *Les Éolides*; choral: *Ruth*	Liszt, Alkan
Garner, Errol	1921 - 1977	United States	Modern	Many jazz piano solos: *Misty, Laura, Dreamy, Solitaire, Errol's Bounce, Blues Garni*	Brubeck, Shearing
Gershwin, George	1898 - 1937	United States	Modern	Piano concerto: *Rhapsody in Blue*; orchestra: *An American in Paris*; operas: *Porgy and Bess*	Ives, Coward
Glazunov, Alexander	1865 - 1936	Russia	Late Romantic	Ballets: *Raymonda*, nine symphonies, violin concerto, two piano concertos, orchestra: *The Sea*	Liszt, Gliere
Gliere, Reinhold	1875 - 1926	Russia	Late Romantic	Ballets: *The Red Poppy*, three symphonies, 123 songs, *March of the Red Army* for wind orchestra	Glazunov, Skryabin
Gluck, Christoph W.	1714 - 1787	Germany	Classical	Operas: *Orfeo ed Euridice*; ballets: *Don Juan*; opéras - comiques: *La Rencontre Imprévue*	Vivaldi, Piccinni
Godard, Benjamin	1849 - 1895	France	Romantic	Piano: *12 Études Artistiques, Lanterne Magique*; operas: *La vivandière*; orchestra: *Oriental Symphony*	Franck, Alkan
Goosens, Sir Eugene	1893 - 1962	England	Modern	Chamber music, choral works, orchestra: oboe concerto, *Sinfonietta*	Benjamin, Stravinsky
Grainger, Percy	1882 - 1961	Australia	Late Romantic	Piano: *In a Nutshell, Hill Songs* Nos. 1 and 2; piano folk song settings: *Country Gardens*	Delius, Grieg
Granados, Enrique	1867 - 1916	Spain	Late Romantic	Operas: *María del Carmen, Goyescas*; piano: *10 Spanish Dances*	Albeniz, Falla
Grechaninov, Alexander	1864 - 1956	Russia	Late Rom/ Modern	Orchestra: *Concert Overture in D minor*, String Quartet Op. 2; operas: *Dobrïnya Nikitich*; liturgies	Gliere, Glazunov
Grieg, Edvard	1843 - 1907	Norway	Late Romantic	Piano: five albums of *Lyric Pieces, Humoresques*; piano concerto; orchestra: *Peer Gynt Suite, In Autumn*	Grainger, Delius
Gurlitt, Cornelius	1820 - 1901	Germany	Romantic	Keyboard: *Album for the Young* Op. 140, many sonatinas, operas, cantatas, symphonies	Schumann, Liszt
Handel, George Frederick	1685 - 1759	Germany	Baroque	Oratorios: *The Messiah, Israel in Egypt*; orchestra: *Water Music, Music for Royal Fireworks*; operas: *Rinaldo*; harpsichord: eight suites, six fugues	Bach, Purcell
Haydn, Joseph	1732 - 1809	Austria	Classical	104 symphonies: No. 104 (*London*), oratorios: *The Creation*; piano sonatas, string quartets	Mozart, Beethoven
Heller, Stephen	1813 - 1888	Hungary	Romantic	Piano: *Studies* Op. 25, *Preludes* Op. 81, 119, 150, *Quatre Barcarolles* Op. 141, *Ballades* op. 121;	Schumann, Liszt
Henschel, Sir George	1850 - 1934	Germany	Romantic	Operas: *Nubia*; 20 piano pieces, songs, sacred choral music, string quartets	Brahms, Strauss
Hindemith, Paul	1895 - 1963	Germany	Modern	Operas: *Mathis der Maler, Cardillac*; concerto for orchestra; small orchestra: *Kammermusik* series	Schoenberg, Bartók
Holland, Dulcie	1913 - 2000	Australia	Modern	*Trio* for violin, cello and piano, *Symphony for Pleasure*, many piano pieces	Hyde, Sutherland

COMPOSER	DATES	BIRTH-PLACE	PERIOD	MAJOR WORKS	CONTEM-PORARIES
Honegger, Arthur	1892 - 1955	Switzer-land	Modern	Psalm: *Le Roi David;* orchestra: *Pacific 231, Symphonie Liturgique, Le chant de Nigamon*	Ibert, Milhaud
Hummel, Johann Nepomuk	1778 - 1837	Austria	Classical/ Romantic	Piano sonatas, concertos, symphonic masses, operas, oratorios, chamber music: *Septet Militaire*	Beethoven, Schubert
Hunter, Glenn	1953 -	Australia	Modern	Piano works: *Birds of Paradise, Magic in the Rainforest, Big Band Blues, The Ragtime Trilogy*	Bailey, Milne
Hutchens, Frank	1892 - 1965	New Zealand	Modern	Two pianos & orchestra: *Fantasie Concerto;* piano: *The Enchanted Isle;* voice/orchestra: *Airmail Palestine*	Grainger, Fuchs
Hyde, Miriam	1913 - 2005	Australia	Modern	Many piano works: *The Grey Forshore, Spring of Joy;* orchestra: *Adelaide Overture;* song: *Elfin Fantasy*	Holland, Sutherland
Ibert, Jacques	1890 - 1962	France	Late Rom/ Modern	Operas: *Angélique;* ballets: *Les Rencontres;* orchestra: *Escales;* chamber music	Honegger, Milhaud
Ireland, John	1879 -1962	England	Romantic/ Modern	Piano solos: *Decorations, Equinox;* chamber and orchestral music, brass band music	Grainger, Williams
Janáček, Leoš	1854-1928	Czecho-slovakia	Romantic/ Modern	operas: *Jenufa;* piano: *Vallachian Dances;* works for chorus, chamber groups, orchestra	Elgar, Delius
Jolivet, André	1905 - 1974	France	Modern	*Trois temps pour piano;* ballets: *Guignol et Pandore;* chamber works: *Trois Complaintes du Soldat*	Messiaen, Varèse
Joplin, Scott	1868 - 1917	United States	Modern/ Ragtime	Piano rags: *The Entertainer, Elite Syncopations, Maple Leaf Rag, The Cascades;* operas: *Treemonisha*	Sousa, Morton
Kabalevsky, Dmitri	1904 - 1987	Russia	Modern	Symphonies, operas: *Colas Breugnon;* 24 preludes for piano, children's songs: *School Days*	Shostakovich, Khachaturian
Kats-Chernin, Elena	1957 -	Uzbek-istan	Modern	Many orchestal and piano works, chamber operas: *Iphis, Matricide*	Edwards, Westlake
Khachaturian, Aram	1903 - 1978	Armenia	Modern	Ballets: *Gayaneh, Spartacus;* piano and violin concertos, symphonies, orchestral suite: *Battle of Stalingrad*	Shostakovich, Stravinsky
Köhler, Christian Louis	1820 - 1886	Germany	Romantic	Many piano studies, operas: *Maria Dolores;* songs, choruses, ballet music	Liszt, Wagner
Krebs, Johann Anton	1713 - 1780	Germany	Classical	Organ pieces: *E Major Toccata;* sacred choral works: *Jesu, meine Freude;* flute sonatas and trios	C.P.E. Bach, Gluck
Kreisler, Fritz	1875 - 1962	Austria	Late Romantic	Violin pieces: *Caprice Viennois, Liebesfreud, Liebeslied;* operetta: *Apple Blossoms;* concerto cadenzas	Kodaly, Hindemith
Kreutzer, Rodolphe	1766 - 1831	France	Classical	Violin pieces: *Études ou Caprices;* 19 violin concertos, 17 string quartets, operas and ballets	Beethoven, Field
Kuhlau, Daniel Frederik	1786 - 1832	Germany	Classical	Many sonatinas for piano, flute pieces, *String Quartet in A minor;* operas: *Lulu*	Beethoven, Hummel
Liszt, Franz	1811 - 1886	Hungary	Romantic	*Faust* Symphony, symphonic poems, piano works: *Hungarian Rhapsodies, B minor Sonata*	Schumann, Wagner
Lutosławski, Witold	1913 - 1994	Poland	Modern	Symphonies, chamber music, concertos: *Concerto for Orchestra;* piano pieces: *Sonata*	Britten, Messiaen
MacDowell, Edward Alexander	1860 - 1908	United States	Late Romantic	Piano concertos, piano miniatures: *Woodland Sketches, Sea Pieces, Fireside Tales;* songs	Joplin, Parker
Martin, Frank	1890 - 1974	Switzer-land	Modern	Operas: *The Tempest;* ballets: *Cinderella;* orchestral works: *Petite Symphonie Concertante*	Schoenberg, Honegger
Martinů, Bohuslav	1890 - 1959	Czecho-slovakia	Modern	Orchestra: *The Angel of Death, Česká rapsódie, Le Jazz;* piano works, concertos, operas: *Julietta*	Debussy, Stravinsky
Mendelssohn, Felix	1809 - 1847	Germany	Romantic	Orchestra: overture to *A Midsummer Night's Dream, Italian Symphony; Violin Concerto in E minor*	Chopin, Schumann

COMPOSER	DATES	BIRTH-PLACE	PERIOD	MAJOR WORKS	CONTEM-PORARIES
Messiaen, Olivier	1908 - 1992	France	Modern	*Turangalîla* Symphony, Chamber music: *Quartet for the End of Time*; piano: *Regards sur l'Enfant Jesus*	Milhaud, Jolivet
Milhaud, Darius	1892 - 1974	France	Modern	Orchestra: *Suite Provençale*; opera: *Esther de Carpentras*; *Scaramouche* for two pianos, choral music	Poulenc, Schoenberg
Milne, Elissa	1967 -	Australia	Modern	Educational piano collections: *Little Peppers* series, *Pepperbox Jazz*	Bailey, Chua
Milne, Lorraine	1946 -	Australia	Modern	Variety of works for students, song collections: *The Fix-It Man*; piano pieces: *Jazzamatazz*	Boyd, Norton
Mompou, Federico	1893 - 1987	Spain	Modern	Mainly piano solos: *Charmes, Suburbis, Songs and Dances*; various works for voice	Honegger, Bartók
Moscheles, Ignaz	1794 - 1870	Czecho-slovakia	Romantic	Piano works: Op. 32: *La Marche d'Alexandre, Sonate Mélancolique* Op. 49 , preludes, piano concertos	Mendelssohn, Chopin
Moszkowski, Moritz	1854 - 1925	Germany	Late Romantic	Piano: many studies, *Spanish Dances* for piano duet; songs, opera, ballet, piano and violin concertos	Henschel, Debussy
Mozart, Wolfgang Amadeus	1756 - 1791	Austria	Classical	Operas: *The Marriage of Figaro*, 41 symphonies, 18 piano sonatas, concertos, orchestral and chamber works, about 40 solo songs	Haydn, Beethoven
Norton, Christopher	1953 -	New Zealand	Modern	Variety of works, mainly piano albums for students: *Rock Preludes, Microjazz Collection*	Wedgwood, Milne
Pachelbel, Johann	1653 - 1706	Germany	Baroque	Organ music, orchestra: *Canon in D major*; 78 choral preludes, religious music: *Magnificat*	Muffat, Corelli
Paganini, Niccolò	1782 - 1840	Italy	Romantic	Violin concertos: *La Campanella* from concerto No. 2, solo violin pieces: 24 caprices, *Duo in C*	Kreutzer, Rossini
Paradies, Pietro D.	1707 - 1791	Italy	Late Baroque	Several operas, 12 harpsichord sonatas including famous *Toccata* from Sonata in A	Galuppi, Gluck
Poulenc, Francis	1899 - 1963	France	Modern	Concertos, chamber music, operas, many piano works: Impromptus, ballet: *Les Biches*	Milhaud, Jolivet
Prokofiev, Sergei	1891 - 1953	Russia	Late Rom/Modern	Seven symphonies, nine piano sonatas, chamber works, operas: *Cinderella*; ballet: *Romeo and Juliet*	Shostakovich, Myaskovsky
Purcell, Henry	1659 - 1695	England	Baroque	Stage music: *Dido and Aeneas*; 100 secular songs, cantatas, church music, keyboard works	Pachelbel, Corelli
Quantz, Johann J.	1697 - 1773	Germany	Baroque	300 flute concertos, sonatas, about 200 other works for flute	Handel, Telemann
Rachmaninov, Sergei	1873 - 1943	Russia	Late Romantic	Three operas: *Aleko*; orchestral works, four piano concertos, chamber music, songs: *Vocalise*	Glazunov, Skryabin
Rameau, Jean-Philippe	1683 - 1764	France	Baroque	Many harpichord suites, ballets, operas: *Hippolyte et Aricie*; opera ballets: *Les Indes Galantes*	Montéclair, Bach
Ravel, Maurice	1875 - 1937	France	Impress-ionist	Operas, ballets, chamber music, piano music: *Sonatine, Miroirs*; orchestra: *Boléro, La Valse*	Debussy, Stravinsky
Reger, Max	1873 - 1916	Germany	Late Romantic	Piano pieces, chamber music, choral works, organ pieces, orchestral works: *Sinfonietta*	Mahler, Schoenberg
Rimsky-Korsakov, Nikolai	1844 - 1908	Russia	Late Romantic	Three symphonies, symphonic Suite: *Sheherazade*; songs, 15 operas: *The Snow Maiden, Sadko*	Tchaikovsky, Borodin
Rollin, Catherine	1952 -	United States	Modern	Over 200 pedagogical works, mainly for piano: *Autumn Mood, Creepy Crocodile, Dreams*	Alexander, Bastien
Rózsa, Miklós	1907 - 1995	Hungary	Modern	Orchestral pieces, chamber music, film scores: *Ben Hur*; ballet: *Ballet Hungarica*	Barber, Messiaen

COMPOSER	DATES	BIRTH-PLACE	PERIOD	MAJOR WORKS	CONTEM-PORARIES
Saint-Saëns, Charles Camille	1835 - 1921	France	Late Romantic	Symphonies: *Organ Symphony*; opera: *Samson and Delilah*, piano concertos, organ concerto, six *Bagatelles*	Fauré, Franck
Sarasate, Pablo de	1844 - 1908	Spain	Late Romantic	Transcriptions of Spanish dances, violin works: *Zigeunerweisen, Jota*; two violins: *Navarra*	Bruch, Saint-Saëns
Satie, Erik	1866 - 1925	France	Late Romantic	Works for stage, orchestra, voice, many piano pieces: *Trois Gymnopédies, Trois Gnossiennes*	Debussy, Ravel
Scarlatti, Alessandro	1660 - 1725	Italy	Baroque	Many operas, oratorios, 10 masses, over 600 solo cantatas, 19 serenatas, madrigals, concertos	Corelli, Vivaldi
Scarlatti, Domenico	1685 - 1757	Italy	Baroque	Church music, many keyboard pieces: approx 600 harpsichord 'sonatas', 12 concerto grossi	Bach, Vivaldi
Schmelzer, Johann H.	1630 - 1680	Austria	Baroque	Ballets, Nuptial Mass, vocal works, three volumes of chamber music: *Trio Sonatas*	Purcell, Corelli
Schmitz, Manfred	1939 - 2014	Germany	Modern	Popular pieces for strings: *A Little Pop Music* for cello; piano pieces: *Youth Album for Piano*	Sitsky, Stockhausen
Schoenberg, Arnold	1874 - 1951	Austria	Modern	Orchestral works: *Transfigured Night*; songs, concerto for violin, *Three Piano Pieces* Op. 11	Stravinsky, Ravel
Schubert, Franz Peter	1797 - 1828	Austria	Romantic	About 600 songs, chamber music, nine symphonies, piano: sonatas, impromptus, *Moments Musicaux*	Beethoven, Czerny
Schumann, Robert Alexander	1810 - 1856	Germany	Romantic	Piano works: *Carnaval, Kinderszenen*; four symphonies, concertos, chamber music, song cycles	Liszt, Mendelssohn
Sculthorpe, Peter	1929 - 2014	Australia	Modern	Orchestral works: *Sun Music*; eight string quartets, choral music, piano music: *Sonatina*	Brumby, Williamson
Shearing, George	1919 - 2011	England	Modern	Jazz solos: *Lullaby of Birdland*; many arrangements: *Anastasia, How About You*	Arnold, Andersen
Shostakovich, Dmitri	1906 - 1975	Russia	Modern	15 symphonies, 15 string quartets, sonatas, 24 preludes and fugues, operas: *Lady Macbeth of Mtsensk*	Prokofiev, Khachaturian
Sibelius, Jean	1865 - 1957	Finland	Late Romantic	Seven symphonies, tone poems: *Finlandia*; piano solos, orchestral works, violin concerto, songs	Ravel, Strauss
Sitsky, Larry	1934 -	China	Modern	One ballet, orchestral and chamber music, songs, piano music, operas: *The Golem, Fiery Tales*	Sculthorpe, Brumby
Skryabin (Scriabin), Alexander	1872 - 1915	Russia	Romantic/ Modern	Many études, symphonies, works for piano: concerto, 10 sonatas, sets of preludes	Glière, Glazunov
Smetana, Bedřich	1824 - 1884	Czecho-slovakia	Romantic	Several operas: *Bartered Bride*; choral works, orchestral works, piano music: three polkas, Czech dances	Liszt, Dvořák
Solal, Martial	1927 -	France	Modern	Jazz piano solos: *Jordu, Gavotte à Gaveau, Jazz Preludes*	Bastien, Berio
Spohr, Ludwig (or Louis)	1784 - 1859	Germany	Classical/ Romantic	Nine symphonies, violin concertos, operas: *Faust;* 36 quartets, trios for violin, piano music	Clementi, Weber
Stamitz, Johann W.A.	1717 - 1757	Czecho-slovakia	Classical	Over 50 symphonies, 10 orchestral trios, violin concertos, chamber music, violin sonatas	Gluck, C.P.E. Bach
Stravinsky, Igor	1882 - 1971	Russia	Modern	Symphonies, ballet music: *The Rite of Spring, The Firebird*; operas, piano music	Schoenberg, Ravel
Strayhorn, Billy (William)	1915 - 1967	United States	Modern	Many jazz piano solos: *Take the A Train, After All, Passion Flower, Mid Riff*	Ellington, Gillespie
Suk, Josef	1874 - 1935	Czecho-slovakia	Late Romantic	Orchestral music, variety of chamber music, choral works and piano pieces	Novák, Strauss
Sutherland, Margaret Ada	1897 - 1984	Australia	Modern	Opera, orchestral music, variety of chamber music and piano music	Glanville-Hicks, Holland

COMPOSER	DATES	BIRTH-PLACE	PERIOD	MAJOR WORKS	CONTEM-PORARIES
Takemitsu, Toru	1930 - 1996	Japan	Modern	Various instrumental works: *Gitimalya* (marimba and orchestra), piano: *Far Away, Undisturbed Rest*	Akutagawa, Irino
Tartini, Giuseppe	1692 - 1770	Italy	Baroque	Over 100 violin concertos, violin sonatas: *Devil's Trill Sonata;* symphonies, church music	Telemann, Scarlatti
Tchaikovsky, Pyotr	1840 - 1893	Russia	Romantic	10 operas, six symphonies, piano concertos, violin concerto, string quartets, piano pieces, ballets	Dvořák, Borodin
Tcherepnin, Alexander	1899 - 1977	Russia	Modern	Sonatas, smaller piano works, three operas, four symphonies, five piano concertos, chamber music	Khachaturian, Shostakovich
Telemann, Georg Philipp	1681 - 1767	Germany	Baroque	Passions, operas, orchestral suites, concertos, chamber music, many keyboard pieces	Handel, Bach
Tyner, McCoy	1938 -	United States	Modern	Compositions for jazz quartet: albums: *Real McCoy, Uptown/Downtown, What's New?*	Coltrane, Henderson
Urquhart-Jones, David	1930 -	Scotland	Modern	Variety of educational albums, mainly for piano: *Straight & Jazzy, Moovin' 'N Groovin'*	Brubeck, Brandman
Vaughan Williams, Ralph	1872 - 1958	England	Modern	Stage works, symphonies, orchestral, band, choral, arrangements of English folksongs	Delius, Holst
Veracini, Antonio	1659 - 1733	Italy	Baroque	Variety of violin pieces: sonata for two violins and cello with bass, organ sonatas	Scarlatti, Vivaldi
Vieuxtemps Henri	1820 - 1881	Belgium	Romantic	Seven violin concertos, works for violin and piano, three cadenzas for Beethoven's violin concerto	Spohr, Alkan
Vine, Carl	1954 -	Australia	Modern	Works for stage, film, television, seven symphonies, piano: *Anne Landa Preludes, Red Blues*	Edwards, Sculthorpe
Vivaldi, Antonio	1678 - 1741	Italy	Baroque	Operas, oratorios, church music, sinfonias, sonatas, numerous concertos: *The Four Seasons*	Scarlatti, Bach
Weber, Carl Maria von	1786 - 1826	Germany	Classical	Four piano sonatas, lieder, cantatas, two piano concertos, two symphonies, operas: *Der Freischütz*	Beethoven, Hummel
Wedgwood, Pamela	1947 -	England	Modern	Many albums of contemporary piano pieces for students: *Jazzin' About* series	Norton, Bastien
Wieniawski, Henryk	1835 - 1880	Poland	Romantic	Mazurkas, études, caprices, two violin concertos, and other works	Tchaikovsky, Rimsky-Korsakov
Williamson, Malcolm	1931 - 2003	Australia	Modern	Works for orchestra, chamber, voice, piano and organ, ballet, opera: *Our Man in Havana*	Sculthorpe, Brumby

No matter which composer you are researching, don't just rely on a single website (e.g. Wikipedia). Always verify the information you find by checking multiple resources on the internet.

Also, don't forget to check out the list of print references on page 93, and refer to the BlitzBooks website for up-to-date online resources for musical knowledge.

Your Exam Pieces

←——————————————————→

Use this page to fill out details relating specifically to your practical exam pieces. Your teacher will let you know exactly what is required for your grade and will help you find out the information you need.

You can download more copies of this FREE sheet from **www.blitzbooks.com**

Name of piece: _____

Composer: _____

Meaning of title: _____

_____

Time signature (name and describe):_____

Form: _____ Key:_____

_____

_____

Period of music:_____

Stylistic information:_____

_____

Information on composer's life and works: _____

_____

_____

Checklist: Tick off when you've done this stuff! (Remember to ask your teacher how much you need to know.)

☐ All terms and signs on the music researched and understood

☐ Key, time signature, form and modulations noted and understood

☐ Facts about composer, including contemporaries, researched and memorised

☐ All markings except for fingerings/bowings/breath marks rubbed out

For Parents: Practical Exam Survival Kit

★ Keep information about each piece on hand and close to the music for easy referral.

★ Test your child on all the terms and signs on the page. This is especially helpful if you don't know anything about music... make sure your child explains it so you can understand it!

★ Remind your child to start 'cramming' well before the big day - avoid trying to learn new info about the music while driving to the actual exam!

★ Make sure all pencil marks (except fingering, breathing and bow markings) are rubbed out well before the day of the exam.

★ For parents of non-pianists: if the accompanist has the piano music, make sure your child has an extra copy of the piano accompaniment to study from at home. Musical knowledge questions may be asked from the piano part.

★ If your child intends to play without music in the exam, make sure he/she PRACTISES without the music.

★ Pack all music (including piano accompaniments) into the bag the night before - it must still be taken to the exam even if playing from memory.

★ Encourage performances of the pieces 'concert style' at home.

★ If you need to organise an accompanist, do this at least one month before the exam date; it's important to allow time to find someone and then to be able to have two or three rehearsals.

ANSWERS TO PAGES 6 AND 7

(i)   Brace

(ii)   It's an anacrusis

(iii)   The metronome marking: 60 crotchets per minute

(iv)   Tie

(v)   Accidentals

(vi)   Mezzo staccato - moderately short and detached

(vii)   Barline

(viii)   Fermata; pause sign

(ix)   It tells the player to 'arpeggiate' or 'fan' the chord

(x)   Repeat from the beginning

Suggested Study References

PRINTED RESOURCES

There are a zillion books on music history and musical terms... here are a few of our favourites! Many of them are now available as multimedia resources.

TITLE	AUTHOR
The Oxford Dictionary of Music	Edited Kennedy, M.
A History of Western Music	Grout, Donald J.
Music: An Appreciation (11th Edition)	Kamien, R.
The Oxford Companion to Music	Edited Scholes, P.
The New Grove Dictionary of Music and Musicians	Edited Sadie, S.
Pocket Manual of Musical Terms. 5th Edition	Edited Baker, T.
From Blues to Bop and Beyond... An Overview of Modern Musical Styles for the Student	Cytrynowski, A.
The Student's Dictionary of Musical Terms	Greenish, A.
Essential Dictionary of Music (2nd Edition)	Harnsberger, L.C.
Rudiments of Music	Macpherson, S.

ONLINE RESOURCES:

Check out **www.blitzbooks.com** for a great list of online resources.

Index

←———————————→

You will find the main index entry in **bold** for each listing below. If there are no bold listings it means that all of the page references are of equal importance.

N.B. Composers and Italian/French/German terms are not indexed. You can find these listed alphabetically in Chapter 5 (translations of terms) and Chapter 8 (composers).